Grandfather's Wisdom

Good, old-fashioned advice, handed down
through the ages

Grandfather's Wisdom

Barry Robb

Michael O'Mara Books Limited

First published in Great Britain in 2010 by
Michael O'Mara Books Limited
9 Lion Yard
Tremadoc Road
London SW4 7NQ

A CIP catalogue record for this book is available from the British Library.

Papers used by Michael O'Mara Books Limited are natural, recyclable products
made from wood grown in sustainable forests. The manufacturing processes
conform to the environmental regulations of the country of origin.

ISBN: 978-1-84317-468-4

1 2 3 4 5 6 7 8 9 10

www.mombooks.com

Illustrations by David Woodroffe

Cover design by Joanne Omigie

Designed and typeset by K DESIGN, Somerset

Printed and bound in Great Britain by Clays Ltd, St Ives plc

Contents

The Great Outdoors

Let Play Commence!

A Grandfather's Job

This book is dedicated to grandfathers everywhere – and the grandchildren who keep them young at heart.

SPECIAL ACKNOWLEDGEMENT

Acknowledgements are made to my grandchildren: Cameron, Rebecca and Craig; Eleanor, Jennifer and Abigail; Karl and Daniel; Chloe, Samuel and David, whose contributions made this book possible.

Introduction

Grandfather's Wisdom is a very special thing. Not everyone has it: you can be as old as the hills and still never get it, in fact you don't have to be that old to have it ... only that fortunate group of men who have the 'secret ingredient' can really be deemed to have it. And the secret ingredient is? A grandchild or grandchildren, of course.

Getting it right

Becoming a grandfather brings a whole new range of experiences into your life. You have the opportunity of establishing new relationships that will enrich your own life and give you the privilege of helping, in some degree, to shape the lives of your grandchildren, no matter what age they are or how near or far away from you they live. There are no set rules on 'grandfatherhood' – each grandpa is different yet each has something to offer. What we all have in common is the experience of having brought up our own children and the wisdom that life brings with it. Put these two together and, with a bit of luck, we have a recipe for getting it right – most of the time.

True wisdom

In this book you will find lots of practical hints and tips on doing things in the 'old-fashioned' way. What I've tried to capture is a mixture of sage, well-tested advice that I learned as a youngster from my own ancestors, together with the life lessons one picks up along the way. These life lessons vary from how to mend a china cup to how to inspire respect and self-reliance in younger people, so you could say that Grandfather's Wisdom is a very broad and wide-ranging subject. Whatever you say though, I hope you find some gems of advice mixed in with this grandfather's personal experience, and that it makes you smile every now and again – because that's at the very heart of it.

Doing Things Grandfather's Way

On the surface, 'Grandad's way' may seem irrelevant, old-fashioned or even quaint, but it's based on values that were passed down to him from his father and grandad. These are aspects of life that can't be measured by targets or ticking boxes but concern those elusive qualities that make the difference in life between truly living and merely existing. They should be carefully guarded and nurtured – or they may share the same fate as the dodo.

While doing it Grandad's way may seem out of touch with present-day reality, there are nonetheless certain truths that will always endure. When I was young we didn't have Health and Safety regulations to worry about, as we do today, we just used good, practical common sense. In our neighbourhood there was a real community spirit, which often helped to see people through difficult times. Of course, now and again neighbours disagreed, sometimes passionately, but if there was hardship or anyone required help, it was always forthcoming.

Some old practices and pastimes with their own rules and ethics will inevitably disappear, and many have already done so, reflecting changes to our society. No doubt the gap will be filled by new rules and codes of behaviour as a result of new technology and changes to society in a world that gets ever smaller and less insular. Nonetheless, some of the mores of yesteryear are as relevant today – and tomorrow – as they have ever been, and if passed on and practised, could lead to a more cohesive society and a happier life.

The days of chivalry

It never ceases to amaze me how disarming a little politeness and a warm smile can be but, regrettably, many of the old practices of courtesy – once taken for granted – are disappearing. When courtesy is offered it is only polite to acknowledge it warmly in the same way. Recently, a young schoolboy stood aside for me to pass and responded to my smile and 'thank you' with his own warm smile and a very pleasant, 'You're welcome!' That simple exchange made my day. Chivalry does still exist – you might need to search a bit harder to find it, but it's worth it!

The changing roles of men and women

When I got married in the 1950s the roles of men and women were more clearly defined. The wife would be expected to have a drink and a meal prepared for her husband when he returned from work, and an ear ready to listen to the highs and lows of his day. Working mothers – let alone single mothers – were very much in the minority.

Now, male and female roles are interchangeable, with many women being the joint breadwinner – sometimes the sole breadwinner. In the home, the household tasks are now usually shared, with the wife being just as adept at changing a plug as her husband is at changing a nappy (unheard of in Grandpa's day!). The equality of women has often been used as a reason for the decline in courtesy. There are women who believe that a male act of courtesy towards them somehow demeans their status. For me, courtesy is a part of life and whatever your gender it should be forthcoming and appreciated. Moreover the consideration shown to the female sex (sometimes called 'old world charm') should be cherished and appreciated, not criticized or derided.

'Manners are caught not taught'

This old saying contains far more wisdom than the conflicting advice 'Do as I say and not as I do'. You have only to observe young children playing to realize that, at a very early age, the language and actions used in their play mimics what they see in the home or at nursery. For this reason it is important that parents, grandparents and other carers appreciate the importance of their positions as role models at all times.

The way we treat each other is reflected in the behaviour of our children. If we treat them courteously, then hopefully it will catch on. Sadly, it becomes increasingly difficult to find time for common courtesies towards each other. This lack of consideration makes us less tolerant of each other as we rush about, always thinking of the next deadline we have to meet.

It is often the case when holding a door open for someone that a stream of people will sweep through quite oblivious to you standing there, and certainly offering no acknowledgement at all. Politeness costs nothing and if we all became practitioners it would be a much more pleasant world for us all to live in.

The three 'Rs'

Respect

The first of the three, respect for oneself and for others, is one of the most important lessons any parent or grandparent can teach a child. Learned while young, respect will serve them well throughout their life.

SELF-RESPECT

Growing up today is very different from years ago. Now children and teenagers are subjected to pressures from every angle – from their peers at school, what they see on TV and on the Internet, in magazines – everywhere. They live in a culture where 'image' seems to be everything, and in which not 'fitting in' can create problems that, if left to fester, can lead to feelings of low self-esteem and a loss of self-respect.

It's important to be able to distinguish between what might be a child's mood swing or some real problem in their life that they are struggling to cope with. If you enjoy a relaxed open relationship with your grandchildren, where they know that they can confide in you and discuss anything with you (without shocking you), then you may be able to gently guide them into putting things into perspective so that they can begin to sort out their own problems, whatever they might be. Try to lend a sympathetic ear and always strictly respect confidences.

Sometimes it's easier for a grandad to do this than it might be for a parent or carer. Life experience and having the time to sit and listen to your grandchild can make a huge difference.

RESPECT FOR OTHERS

We all have an obligation to show respect for others, and an even bigger obligation to foster the spirit of mutual respect in our children. Respect all people as individuals and treat them as you would like to treated. Be tolerant of their differences and avoid being judgemental. We all need to re-examine our attitudes and prejudices from time to time and the way we often 'pigeon-hole' people instead of appreciating them for what they are.

If you can show your children that you have respect for others – whoever they are – you will be giving them a very valuable lesson in life.

RESPECT FOR THE ENVIRONMENT

Everyone says they hate to see people dropping litter, but how often have you been walking down the street and seen somebody casually drop whatever rubbish they happen to be holding? It's infuriating! Litter, vandalism and graffiti have become a way of life for some, with town centres, parks and even parts of the countryside being spoilt by just a few people. Thoughtless acts by the minority blight the lives of others, as well as damaging the environment, thereby affecting everyone's enjoyment. Be litter-conscious and accept a 'zero tolerance' attitude on this matter from the younger generation, then hopefully we'll all take a step in the right direction.

Ways to help reduce littering

- Provide plenty of waste bins in the house.
- Have a waste bag in the car.
- Play 'spot the litter bin' game when out with young children.
- Make recycling fun.
- Set targets and have a reward chart.
- Organize a litter pick around your garden or local green area (supervise, of course, and provide gloves).

RESPECT FOR THE PLANET

These days, many youngsters are very conscious of the damage being done to the planet, and through school and community projects are making enormous efforts to safeguard its future. They could – and do – teach parents and grandparents a lesson by example. We should all become more environmentally aware and look to the success of other countries in this area.

The length of time a human being lives on this planet is minuscule in the great scheme of things. Nevertheless, we need to remember that for that short time we are custodians of the planet: our actions determine the state of the planet for future generations.

Working together to save our planet

Have a look at the following ways to help save the planet *and* save money!

Water conservation

❋ Recycle rainwater – Collect in water butts or, for a new house, consider rainwater harvesting in an underground tank to be used for toilets, washing machine and garden (can halve water consumption).

❋ Take showers instead of baths (doesn't dry the skin).

❋ When cleaning teeth, don't leave the water running – turn the tap off.

❋ Wash dishes and vegetables in a small bowl (can be recycled on the garden).

❋ In the garden, use water sparingly – use mulch to retain water.

Energy conservation

- Get proper insulation for your home.
- Use low-energy light bulbs and appliances.
- Use appliances economically.
- Switch off lights when not in use.
- Don't leave appliances on standby – get up and turn the TV off when you've finished watching.
- Programme heating economically.
- Always fully load your washing machine or dishwasher – two half-loads use much more energy than one full one.
- Turn thermostats down a notch – and wear a jumper instead!
- Keep outside doors closed to retain heat.

Responsibility

Advances in technology have meant that the jobs and tasks we used to do to help out around the house are very different now. Do you know a child who sweeps out the fire in the morning? Or helps Mum with the mangle after doing the washing? Or beats the rug hung over the washing line? We used to do lots of jobs like this and I think it helped me realize, given all the other responsibilities my parents had, just how valuable my parents were to me!

When old enough, children should be made aware that they are responsible for their actions and the consequences of them. Shouldering responsibilities and taking pride in their work will give them an awareness of 'doing their bit' and the part they play within the family, and also help to prepare them for the responsibilities of adult life. Children love having responsibilities and from early on can be given tasks to suit their age such as:

- Tidying their bed
- Folding their clothes
- Putting their toys away

- Helping younger children
- Preparing school bags
- Being responsible for a plot of garden
- Cleaning shoes
- Laying and clearing the table
- Preparing simple meals

Restraint

IMPULSIVE BEHAVIOUR

Most people have at one time or another made impulsive decisions that they have lived to regret. You can't turn back the clock, but you can help your grandchildren to weigh up their judgements so that they are better equipped than you were to make informed decisions.

When trying to make a 'big' decision, it helps to:

- Make a table of pros and cons.
- Weigh them up.
- If the decision involves others, discuss it with them.
- Take your time (if you have it).

- Sleep on it.
- Revisit your decision.
- Make sure you are clear-headed when you finally make your decision.

MANAGING ANGER

Everyone gets annoyed from time to time: children have tantrums, adults lose their tempers. Grandfathers should show their grandchildren by example how they restrain themselves when they are angry.

It helps to:

- Step aside from the situation until you are calm.
- Count to ten before you react.
- Take a deep breath.
- Think rationally.
- Be fair.
- When calmer, find out the facts that led up to the situation.

Courtesies that are almost lost in time

Here are a few of the old-fashioned courtesies that were prevalent when I was young.

- ✁ When walking with a female companion, a man should always walk on the kerbside. This is an old custom going back to the days of unmade muddy roads when the passage of carriages could splash your companion's dress, so in walking on the kerbside you were protecting her. It is an old courtesy that is still practised today to some extent and is much appreciated, particularly on a rainy day when traffic can cause a similar problem.

- ✁ Hats off was the norm for any male entering someone else's house, a church, school or public building – indeed it was considered bad manners not to do so. This is not common practice now, perhaps because hats are no longer as popular as they once were, but it's always a pleasure to see it when it does happen.

- ✁ Touching or lifting (called doffing) one's hat or cap on greeting a female. There are still a few older gentlemen around who display this act of courtesy.

- ✁ When dining, a man would draw out a chair for a lady to sit down and do the same again when she is ready to leave.

- ✁ Offering your seat to any lady, not just the elderly, expectant mothers or people with disabilities.

- Standing up on being introduced or when your hostess enters the room.

Etiquette

This word has almost disappeared from the English language but it covers the customs governing behaviour regarded as acceptable in social or official life, recognizing that there are cultural differences. Of course we live in a dynamic society and rightly things do change but we can regret the passing of some old practices if they reduce the quality and richness of life.

Letter writing

Letter writing is a skill that is in danger of dying out completely, being replaced by emailing and texting. However there are some letters that should still be written by hand. Thank-you letters for birthday and Christmas presents, special occasion gifts, or in appreciation of hospitality are always highly appreciated, and a handwritten letter of condolence is an absolute must.

It's always a pleasure to receive a handwritten thank-you note, which confirms that the effort of choosing and sending a present was

worthwhile. It is an added bonus if the child has gone to the bother of making a home-made card just for you. That would certainly deserve its place in the memory box.

At birthdays and Christmas it is useful to make lists of the presents received to avoid the embarrassment of thanking someone for the wrong present. Children should be encouraged to write and to take a pride in the presentation of their work, illustrating the letter for an extra treat. Of course, letters to Santa are willingly written and usually sent, unbeknown to the writer, to Grandpa, who replies from the 'North Pole' with promises of at least *some* of the requests being delivered on Christmas Eve. (Sometimes it's worth a letter to the Tooth Fairy who just might forget to look under the pillow on that special night.)

Meeting people

Remember there is never a second chance to create a good first impression, so, whether formal, informal or introducing oneself, the approach has common elements.

- ❀ The handshake should be firm and not limp like a wet fish.

- ❀ Make eye contact with the person to whom you are being introduced. Remember, your eyes are one of your greatest assets when you are meeting someone for the first time.

- ❀ Smile to show how pleased you are to meet them (your smile is another valuable asset).

- In a group, always introduce the youngest person first to the oldest person.
- When introducing oneself it is acceptable to give either the first name or the first and second name or just a nickname, depending on the circumstances.

After introductions have been made conversation takes place. The art of good conversation entails listening just as much as talking. Listen with obvious interest and attention before commenting and putting forward your own views. In relaxed situations chatting comes more naturally. When in an already established group, make an effort to include any newcomers into the conversation so that they don't feel left out.

Shaking hands

Making a good first impression is very important whatever you're doing. Be it a straightforward introduction or a more formal situation – like a job interview or an important family occasion, if you have to shake hands with someone, do it right.

There are three steps to a good handshake:

- First make eye contact, smile and say 'hello'.
- Extend your right hand and grip the other person's hand firmly (not squeezing it, just holding it firmly) for three or four seconds.

- Shake hands using your forearm only – not your upper arm or shoulder.

On first introductions, don't be tempted to cover his or her hand with your other hand, this is seen as over-familiar, so only use that for close friends. Always try to ensure your hand isn't damp or sweaty.

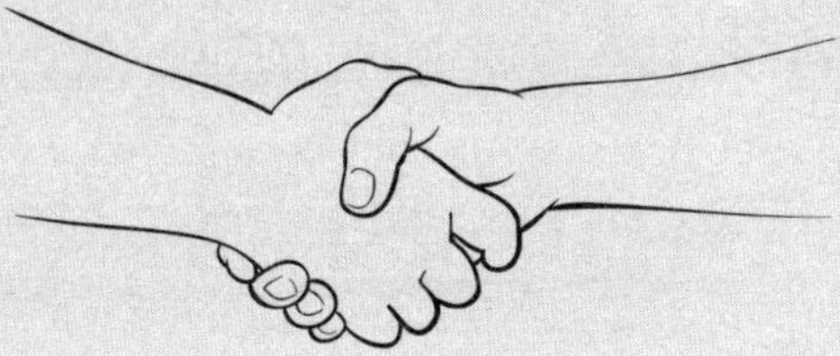

The telephone

Today the telephone is taken for granted, yet I was in my late teens before we had a phone at home: they were just not part of our lives. These days we find it hard to imagine life without a mobile – imagine what it was like without a landline! Nowadays most children have grown up with the telephone and from an early age have become accustomed to answering the phone.

The way in which the telephone is answered can create a good or bad impression, so it's useful to teach your child a good telephone manner. The tone of your voice can indicate the warmth of the welcome to the caller. Be polite and speak clearly, asking who is calling. If the caller asks who you are, say 'Mrs X's son' or, if at your grandpa's, 'Mr Y's granddaughter'.

At the table

In this day and age, with all the rushing about and the distraction of computers, iPods and meals in front of the television, families eat together less frequently, yet a family meal should be a highlight of the day, the bonding time that holds families together. It is a wonderful opportunity to discuss the day's events, current affairs or arrange the diary for the next few days.

Passing the food to others before serving oneself and only starting to eat when everyone has been served, is simply good manners. Having eaten enough, placing your knife and fork together on your plate indicates that you have finished.

In a restaurant or at a formal dinner the array of cutlery can be disconcerting but if you remember to start by using the cutlery furthest away from your plate as each course is served, then it's plain sailing.

Coming through!

When you are walking down the street in a group and see people coming towards you, do the polite thing and step aside or go into single file and let them pass without having to walk in the road.

Oh yuck!

One of the things I hate most is when people spit out chewing gum in the street. Spitting itself is bad enough, but chewing gum on the sole of the shoe is nasty, let alone the horrible mess it leaves on pavements. There are countries where chewing gum is almost completely banned and others where disposing of it in the street will get you fined. That might seem a bit extreme, but really, it's a disgusting and unsavoury habit and we should make sure our youngsters know that.

Old-fashioned values

I'm not going to harp on about the 'youth of today' as very often they can put us oldies to shame! But there are a few 'old-fashioned' rules that are worth remembering:

- Mean what you say and say what you mean – keep your promises and you'll find that others will do the same for you.

- Lead by example – if you are in a position of responsibility, you have or look after children, always remember that your child will learn by looking at what you do – how you treat others, how you communicate your feelings, your values, your integrity etc. Every day your child will learn a little bit more from you. Make sure it's all good stuff.

- Be honest and be aware of the value of honesty and trustworthiness. Explain to your child that liars are not to be believed or trusted.

- Be unselfish and think of others, and encourage your children to put others before him/herself. In these modern times, when everything seems to be handed to us on a plate, it can be difficult to put the needs of others first, but self-control and unselfishness is a key mark of maturity.

- Respect other people and their differences. Good manners and a positive outlook can get you far in this world. If you are respectful towards others, you can expect the same treatment.

- Be a good and loyal friend and try to understand other people's feelings. Standing up for your friends is character building.

- Be fair – know the difference between right and wrong and stick by it.

A maxim to live by

When you've got nothing to say – say nothing! Emails, texting, messaging – it's so easy to communicate these days that often a knee-jerk reply, sent before putting brain into gear, can be fatal to a friendship or in a work scenario. Take, for example, the cases we read about in the newspapers where an 'innocent' email addressed to one person goes viral and suddenly it's national – even global – news?

It's the same in conversation. Very often you hear people jabbering on about a subject on which they obviously have no knowledge at all, or being led down a conversational path that can only lead to embarrassment.

Always try to temper your reactions and responses – not everything needs an immediate reply – think about it and make sure that you really are saying what you mean.

Ethics

The wisdom of proverbs or 'age-old truths' and fables has been passed down from as far back as ancient Greece, the best known being the Fables of Aesop. It is thought he was born a slave in about 620 BC and had extraordinary wisdom but later he became a freed man. He is credited with over six hundred ethical and moral-based stories. The stories, which depict animals that can talk, are often read in primary schools and by parents to their children and grandparents to their grandchildren. They are not only appealing, but also have a message just as relevant in today's world as when Aesop thought them up more than two thousand years ago. I well remember them from my primary school days. Some of these are:

- The Boy Who Cried Wolf – a persistent liar will not be believed even when he is telling the truth

- The Wind and the Sun – persuasion is better than force
- The Fox and the Grapes – it is too easy to despise what you cannot have – sour grapes
- The Fox and the Crow – do not trust flatterers
- The Wolf in Sheep's Clothing – appearances can be deceptive
- The Ant and the Grasshopper – there is a time to work and a time to play
- The Tortoise and the Hare – avoid complacency
- The Dog in the Manger – people often begrudge others what they cannot enjoy themselves
- The Mouse and the Lion – there are times when the weak can help the strong
- The Miser and His Gold – wealth unused might as well not exist

Proverbs that have been passed down through generations are wise sayings but without a story, though many are similar in message to the Fables. Unfortunately they are not used as much as they used to be but they enrich our language and it would be a sad loss to future generations if they got forgotten in time. Here is a small selection:

❉ 'Save your breath to cool your porridge' – stop talking nonsense.

❉ 'Don't judge a book by its cover' – appearances can be deceptive.

❉ 'Don't put off until tomorrow what you can do today' – avoid procrastination.

❉ 'An empty vessel makes the most sound' – inane and empty-headed chatter is indicative of little brain power.

❉ 'Look before you leap' – think before you act.

❉ 'A stitch in time saves nine' – doing the job now will save more work later.

❉ 'A bird in the hand is worth two in the bush' – appreciate what you have already got.

❉ 'Don't count your chickens until they are hatched' – wait until you are sure.

❉ 'If a job's worth doing, it's worth doing well' – whatever you're doing, always give it your best shot.

❉ 'Many hands make light work' – the more people doing a job, the easier it will be.

And always remember: 'To err is human, to forgive divine.'

Grandfather in the Kitchen

The modern man seems very comfortable in the kitchen, often coming home from a day's work and preparing the evening meal, while his wife (also just back from a day's work) deals with the children – homework, bath-time etc. When I was a young husband and father, things didn't work quite like that. Few mothers went out to work (equal pay hadn't even come in then) and the wife had the meal ready when the husband got home and also dealt with all the children's needs. What an easy time we had! Consequently many grandfathers are relative novices in the kitchen.

Realizing the importance of being able to put simple meals on the table I have built up a collection of well-tried favourite recipes that are healthy and inexpensive. I use unprocessed ingredients, fresh seasonal vegetables (from the garden when possible, and no air miles involved). There are no additives in these meals, no salt and minimum amounts of fat and sugar, unlike many convenience foods (if buying the latter it is advisable to check the ingredients on the label). Here are some examples of my culinary repasts!

Breakfast

People often neglect breakfast in their rush to arrive to work or school on time, but a healthy filling breakfast can avoid 'snacking' on sweets and crisps before lunch. If you are preparing a more elaborate breakfast as a special treat, select items that can be grilled rather than fried, such as mushrooms, tomatoes and bacon with beans and a poached or scrambled egg. That way you'll have a healthier start to the day.

Porridge
(serves 2)

I love porridge, and you can add lots of different toppings to 'personalize' your dish. Porridge releases energy slowly and it will set you up until lunchtime.

- ✖ Use 1 cup of porridge oats to 2½ cups of water.

- ✖ Bring to boil stirring all the time.

- ✖ Reduce the heat and simmer until cooked (approximately 3 minutes).

- ✖ Serve with banana or other fruit such as prunes, apple or apricots. Add honey or maple syrup and milk to taste and, if desired, a sprinkle of cinnamon and linseed (rich in omega 3).

Basic muesli
(serves 8 generous portions)

Home-made muesli is another healthy way to start the day. It's simple to prepare and can be made the night before, to save the morning rush. It is worth making a reasonable amount since the dry ingredients can be stored.

> 6 oz (150 g) rolled oats
> 1 oz (25 g) bran
> 1 oz (25 g) wheatgerm
> 2 oz (50 g) bran flakes

Mix the ingredients together. Experiment by using different types of grain and seeds. When serving add a selection of dried fruits such as prunes, apricots, raisins, currants together with some chopped nuts and apple or banana. Fruit juice, milk or low fat yoghurt are excellent accompaniments.

Main meals

All the dishes I've suggested here are all hearty, flavoursome ones that have served me well over the years. Soups and stews make a simple and satisfying meal, so I've put in a few of my favourites.

Carrot and fresh ginger soup
(serves 3 – with second helpings)

> 1 stick of celery
> 2 medium onions
> 2 potatoes
> 675 g (1½ lb) carrots
> 25 g (1 oz) margarine
> 1 tbsp grated fresh root ginger
> 1.2 l (2 pints) chicken or vegetable stock
> 150 ml (¼ pint) single cream
> 1 pinch grated nutmeg
> Seasoning to taste

Chop celery, onions, potatoes and carrots. Put the margarine into a large saucepan, heat and soften the onion and celery in the melted margarine. Add the ginger, potato, carrots and stock and simmer for 20 to 25 minutes, until the vegetables are cooked through.

When cool, use a blender to purée the soup. Warm up again, stir in the cream and nutmeg and serve with a hunk of good wholemeal bread.

Spiced parsnip and apple soup
(serves 3 – with second helpings)

> 40 g (1½ oz) butter
> 1 tbsp groundnut oil or sunflower oil
> 1 onion, chopped
> 2 cloves of garlic, chopped
> 1 tsp ground coriander
> ½ tsp ground cumin
> ½ tsp ground turmeric
> ¼ tsp chilli powder
> 675 g (1½ lb) parsnips, diced
> 1.2 l (2 pints) chicken or vegetable stock
> 1 Bramley apple, grated
> 150 ml (¼ pint) single cream
> Seasoning to taste

Heat the butter and oil in a large saucepan, add the onion and garlic, cooking until softened. Add the spices, cooking for a further minute, then the parsnips. Stir in the stock, add seasoning and simmer until parsnips are tender. After cooling, purée with a blender until smooth. Re-heat to serve, adding the grated apple and the cream. Serve with crusty rolls.

Nettle soup
(serves 4)

Often regarded as a stinging nuisance and a weed to be rid of, nettles were once widely used in tisanes, soup and as a vegetable.

> 450 g (1 lb) young nettle leaves, washed
> 4 onions, chopped
> 2 tbsp butter
> 2 potatoes
> 1 l (2 pints) water
> Cream to decorate
> Salt and pepper to taste

Take one-third of the leaves and chop finely. In a saucepan, combine the chopped onions and the butter and cook until soft. Stir in the whole nettle leaves and cook for one minute. Add the potatoes and water and season. Simmer until the potato is cooked through. Leave the soup to cool, then purée until smooth, add the cream and sprinkle on the chopped nettles and serve with crusty bread.

Kedgeree
(serves 4)

The kedgeree dish – an Indian favourite, but adapted here for younger palates – is mild enough for anyone to enjoy.

> 350 g (12 oz) smoked haddock
> 225 g (8 oz) easy-cook rice
> 25 g (1 oz) butter
> 1 tbsp mild curry powder
> 50 g (2 oz) frozen peas, cooked
> 2 tbsp parsley, chopped
> 3 hard-boiled eggs
> Salt and pepper to taste

Steam, microwave or poach the fish until cooked. Leave it to cool, then break up into large flakes. Cook the rice until tender, adding the liquid in which you cooked the fish to the cooking water. When cooked, drain the rice and put aside. Heat the butter in a large frying pan or wok and add the curry powder, cooking gently for 1 to 2 minutes. Add the fish, rice, peas and most of the parsley to the pan, keeping a half-tablespoon of parsley aside for garnish. Mix and heat together gently. Chop two and slice one of the hard-boiled eggs, and gradually add the chopped eggs to the mixture, stirring continuously until the mixture is thoroughly heated. Serve in a large dish, garnished with the remaining parsley and the sliced egg.

Beef in beer
(serves 4)

This beef recipe is made using a slow cooker, which is especially handy if you are going out for the day and want to return to the tempting aroma of a hot meal just ready to serve. The setting can be adjusted according to the length of time you are going to be away. You can use any of your favourite casserole recipes in a slow cooker. (It's also useful if the whole family is descending on you and you want to spend the time with them rather than over a hot stove in the kitchen.)

> Vegetable oil for frying
> 1 kg (2 lb) braising steak, cut into chunks
> Flour for coating
> Freshly ground black pepper
> 8 shallots or small onions
> 4 celery stalks, thickly sliced
> 2 large carrots, peeled and sliced
> 1 large leek, cut into chunks
> 300 ml (½ pint) beer
> 1 tsp vinegar
> Vegetable stock (as required)
> 1 bouquet garni
> Freshly chopped parsley

Heat 2 tbsp oil in a large frying pan. Coat the steak in the flour seasoned with black pepper and put into the frying pan. Brown on all sides over a high heat, then remove the meat and set aside. Add the vegetables to the frying pan and cook for 5 minutes until lightly coloured, then put the meat and the vegetables into the ceramic cooking pot of the slow cooker. Stir in the beer, vinegar and sufficient vegetable stock to cover the contents of the pot. Add the bouquet garni and chopped parsley and place the cooking pot into the slow cooker and put on the lid. Following the manufacturer's instructions, set the control switch on the slow cooker to the appropriate setting (low, medium or high depending on when you want the meal to be ready).

When you are ready to eat and the slow cooker has done its thing, discard the bouquet garni and serve your warming beef stew with mashed potatoes and a seasonal green vegetable.

Baked apples
(serves 4)

You don't see this classic favourite much any more. I don't know why, a baked apple can make the tastiest dessert, and apart from a bit of sugar, it's good for you, too!

> 4 medium-sized cooking apples
> Selection of chopped, dried fruit
>   (raisins, sultanas, chopped dates etc.)
> 4 tsp soft brown sugar

Scrub and core the apples and, cooking two at a time, place in a microwaveable dish. Stuff the centre of each apple with dried fruit and add a teaspoon of the sugar on top.

Place in microwave and cook for approximately 3 minutes (depending on your microwave – check manufacturer's instructions). When the apple is cooked through and the sugar is melted, leave to cool for a few minutes before serving with ice cream or custard.

Spiced pears with apricots
(serves 4)

Delicious, moreish – and incredibly easy to make.

8 medium-sized ripe pears
200 g (7 oz) dried apricots
½ l apple juice
2 tbsp honey (or to taste)
1 cinnamon stick
8 cloves
1 cardamom pod, lightly crushed
Greek yoghurt, to serve

Halve, peel and core the pears and place them in a medium-sized pan with all the other ingredients. Bring to a boil and gently simmer for 10 minutes or until the fruit is soft. Remove from the heat and leave the mixture to stand so that the spices infuse. If you want to, remove spices (you can leave them in, they do look attractive), then serve, either warm or cold, with Greek yoghurt (and keep any leftovers for a spicy breakfast dish).

Herbs in the kitchen

If you grow, harvest and store your herbs (see pages 121–5), what can you do with them? Lots!

- Make bouquet garni – take a sprig of thyme, a sprig of parsley, a sprig of marjoram and a bay leaf and tie them up with a short piece of cotton like a bouquet. This provides essential flavouring for soups and stews.

- Make a mixture of *fines herbes* – chopped parsley, tarragon, chervil and chives. Unbeatable when sprinkled over a salad.

- Make your favourite mixed herbs – these are usually made with more 'coarse'-flavoured herbs, such as sage, marjoram, parsley and thyme. Grind the dried herbs together and add to lots of savoury dishes, from pastas to pastries.

- Make herb vinegars – for special salad dressings and drizzled into mayonnaise, herb vinegars pack quite a flavoursome punch. Fennel, tarragon, basil and dill are good herbs to use. Pack the herbs into a wide-mouthed jar, bruising them slightly with a wooden spoon. Add warm – not boiled – white wine vinegar and cover the jar tightly. Leave in a warm, dark place for two months, giving the jar a gentle shake every now and then. Drain off the vinegar, bottle it and label with the name of the herb and the date.

- Herb butter – make small pats of chilled herb-flavoured butter to go on steaks, chops and fish. All you have to do is cream 100 g (4 oz) of butter with a fork until it has softened, then add a teaspoon of lemon juice and a couple of tablespoons of chopped, fresh herbs of your choice. Parsley, mint, tarragon and chives are all good. Mix the herbs in with the butter and leave to stand at room temperature for a couple of hours to let the flavours mingle, then store in the fridge until you need it.

What goes with what?

Here's an easy guide to help you decide what herbs go with favourite foods:

- Chicken – parsley, thyme, marjoram, tarragon
- Beef – marjoram, oregano, savory, thyme
- Lamb – rosemary, mint, marjoram, dill, savory
- Pork – sage, marjoram, rosemary
- Veal – rosemary, sage, lemon thyme, savory, lemon balm
- Ham – parsley, sage, marjoram

- Fish – fennel, thyme, chervil, chives, dill, sage, mint, basil, parsley
- Cheese – caraway, basil, chives, dill, mint, sage, tarragon, thyme, marjoram
- Eggs – basil, marjoram, parsley, tarragon, chervil, chives, dill
- Salads – chervil, chives, sage, lemon balm, mint, parsley, tarragon, borage, basil
- Vegetables – rosemary, basil, chives, tarragon, fennel, mint, parsley
- Fruit cocktails – lemon balm, mint, borage, rosemary

A few recipes from the children

Realizing that I could do with a bit more variety in my menus, I often ask the grandchildren for their help when they come to visit. They are only too pleased to lend me a hand in the kitchen, suggesting recipes or providing me with recipes they have used at school that they think might be just up Grandpa's street. Here are a few of them.

Tomato and basil tart

A bit more adventurous perhaps …

> 100 g plain flour
> 50 g butter
> 2–3 tbsp cold water
> 2 tomatoes
> Basil leaves
> 2 eggs
> 125 ml semi-skimmed milk
> 50 g cheese
> Black pepper

Pre-heat oven to 180°C. To make the shortcrust pastry, sift the flour into a bowl and, using your fingertips, rub the butter into the flour until it looks like breadcrumbs. Add the cold water and start to mix together to form a firm, smooth dough. Roll out the pastry on a lightly floured surface, then line a square or circular cake tin with the pastry and trim the edge with a palette knife. Prick the bottom of the pastry with a fork.

To make the filling, slice the tomatoes, grate the cheese and whisk the eggs and milk together. Tear the basil into the mixture and add black pepper. Pour the egg mixture into the pastry shell and arrange the tomato slices and cheese on top.

Then bake for 30 minutes until the pastry is golden and the filling is firm. You should now have a delicious tomato and basil tart.

Savoury slices
(serves 10–12)

This is so easy, but it's a tasty little snack that you can make with the kids – and revel in the pride they feel when the slices come out of the oven!

> 1 sheet puff pastry
> A tube of tomato purée
> Grated cheese

Pre-heat the oven to 200°C. Roll out pastry to about half an inch thick. Spread the tomato purée evenly all over it and sprinkle on the grated cheese. Then roll the whole lot up like a Swiss roll and cut into slices. Put the slices on a pre-heated baking tray and bake in the oven for 8-10 minutes. Enjoy warm – but remember to share!

Special treats

Naughty but nice, the following sweet treats will earn you a few brownie points with the grandkids.

Chocolate chip cookies

> 70 g (2.5 oz) caster sugar
> 70 g (2.5 oz) soft brown sugar
> 115 g (4 oz) butter
> 140 g (5 oz) plain flour
> 1 egg
> ½ tsp bicarbonate of soda
> ½ tsp vanilla essence
> 175 g (6 oz) chocolate chips

Pre-heat oven to 190°C. Mix the butter and both lots of sugar in a mixing bowl until creamy, then break the egg and beat it into the mixture until smooth. Mix in the vanilla essence, and begin to add the flour and bicarbonate of soda a bit at a time. Mix thoroughly. Stir in the chocolate chips until evenly mixed through. Grease two baking trays, and spoon small mounds of the mixture onto the baking trays, leaving sufficient space between each mound for the mixture to 'settle' a little. Bake for 10-12 minutes until the cookies are an even golden-brown colour. When cooked, put the cookies onto a wire rack to cool. These can be stored in an airtight container – if they last that long!

Caramel sauce

I know it's unhealthy; I know it's bad for the teeth. But this sauce is so bad it's good! A touch on a pancake or on some good vanilla ice cream and you cannot go wrong. Grandfather's promise.

> 250 g (8 oz) caster sugar
> 4 tbsp water
> 142 ml (¼ pint) double cream
> 50 g (2 oz) butter

Put the sugar in a large, heavy-based saucepan and add the water. Place on a medium heat until the sugar has dissolved, then turn up the heat and let it bubble for a few minutes until the sugar caramelizes. Take off the heat and carefully stir in the cream and butter until it's all combined well and there are no lumps. Leave to cool and bottle.

Pancakes
(serves 4)

Always a hit with the children, pancakes are a special treat at breakfast time – especially if you are planning an active day to work them off.

> 250 g (8 oz) self-raising flour
> 125 g (4 oz) caster sugar
> pinch of salt
> 2 eggs, beaten
> Milk
> Butter for greasing

Mix together the flour, sugar and salt, then add the well-beaten eggs. Add enough milk to make a thick batter. Heat a well-greased frying pan and carefully drop a dessertspoonful of the batter into the pan. Watch how it settles in the pan, then add another, and another, depending on the size of your frying pan. Cook the pancakes until they are brown on one side, then, when each pancake starts to bubble and rise up, turn or flip it over and cook the other side. When cooked, place on a plate and cover with a tea towel until the next batch is done. Serve with jam, golden syrup or – my favourite – caramel sauce (see above).

Real lemonade

Good traditional lemonade can't be beaten – forget your cans of fizzy drinks, if you want to quench your thirst, this is the drink to do it for you. Adults quite like the zest left in but kids don't generally like it. Always remember to check the sweetness level before serving – but don't overdo it!

> 4 unwaxed lemons
> 100 g caster sugar
> Water

Using a zester or potato peeler, cut away some of the zest of each lemon, trying not to cut into the white pith as this is quite bitter. Then squeeze all four lemons and put the zest and juice in a large jug. Pour over about 500 ml boiling water and stir in the sugar until it has completely dissolved. Leave the mixture to cool and, when cold, strain it through a sieve and discard the zest. Dilute the mixture with a further 500 ml water (preferably chilled) and check for sweetness, adding a little more sugar if desired. Serve chilled with a sprig of mint from your herb garden or a slice of lemon!

The joy of wine

I've enjoyed my fair share of wine over the years, and there are few things more enjoyable than sitting back after a hard day's work – whether at the office or in the garden – and enjoying a drop of what you fancy.

Red or white?

I love reading the headlines that appear to tell us that wine drinking (in moderation) can have health benefits. It makes me feel even more justified in enjoying a glass or two now and then. Apparently red wine is healthier than white because it contains more 'polyphenols', molecules found in plants (grapes) that have antioxidant properties, which in turn help to keep the body's cells in good shape.

The ancient Egyptians used wine as medicine back in 2200 BC, and it has been used in various ways for its medicinal properties ever since, on ailments ranging from bronchitis to dementia; in fact the first printed book on wine was written in the fourteenth century by a physician – so that tells you something!

Wine and food

'White with fish, red with meat' was the saying I always remember. And while there's still some truth in that, there are so many different wines to choose from you would be daft not to be a bit more adventurous sometimes, especially if you only have yourself to please. Basically, you know what you like, but if you have a dinner party coming up or want to get it right for a formal occasion, while Grandma (or Mum) can be in charge of the food, here are a few suggestions for wines that will enhance that meal.

Meat

- Beef – a good rump steak deserves a robust red wine like a Bordeaux to bring out the beefy flavours, whereas for a beef casserole a milder, lighter Burgundy will do nicely.

- Lamb – for older lamb dishes the deep rich flavours of a Bordeaux will bring out the flavours, while a Grenache would be perfect for roast spring lamb.

- Pork – try a full-bodied Rioja for roast pork, but you might find a Chianti more suitable for marinated or barbecued pork.

- Cold meats – with strong-flavoured preserved meats such as salami, try a Pinot Noir or a wine from the Rhône Valley.

- Veal – the whiter the meat, the lighter the wine should be, so often white wines such as Vouvray or Soave are very good served with white veal dishes. For darker meat, try a rich Bordeaux, which will bring out the flavours.

Poultry

- Chicken – try a crisp Chablis with classic roast chicken, and for darker meat try a young red such as Shiraz.

- Turkey – this needs a fuller-bodied wine to bring its flavours out, so go for a Shiraz or a fruity Zinfandel.

- Duck – rich and distinctive in flavour, this bird needs a rich red such as a Rhône or a Burgundy.

Fish

- Trout or salmon – try fresh whites such as Chablis or Riesling to bring out the natural flavours of these fish.

- Haddock, cod and other seawater fish – best served simply – poached and with a squeeze of lemon – a Chardonnay or a White Burgundy will enhance their lemony fresh flavours.

- Oily and smoked fish – smoked salmon? No question: Champagne is the only option! For smoked mackerel, try a crisp Mosel to cut through its strong flavour. For meaty textures and flavours of tuna, swordfish and sardines a Muscadet will be the perfect complement.

- Shellfish – lobster, crab, prawns, shrimp, there's a great variety of shellfish and your choice of wine will depend on how you are cooking them. A fruity Gerwürztraminer will be lovely with simply prepared lobster or crab, whereas you might find a spicy Rioja will be perfect with prawns cooked in a creamy sauce.

Vegetarian dishes

- Pasta – Chianti, of course!

- Rice dishes – for a risotto, make sure the wine you serve is light and crisp – a Pinot Grigio will cut through that creaminess.

✿ Vegetables, nut and bean dishes – roast vegetables are complemented by fuller-bodied reds such as Merlot, but you might find that a more fruity rosé will be just the thing.

A babble about the bubbles

I don't know many people who dislike this heady drink. I read somewhere that an American scientist worked out there are around 49 million bubbles in the average bottle of Champagne – no wonder they call it bubbly! And the bubbles aren't just for show: apparently they get you drunker quicker by helping the alcohol reach the bloodstream faster.

The morning after ...

A hangover is not only caused by the amount of alcohol you drink, but by the preservatives and chemical by-products from the fermentation process – cogeners – in the drinks. The rule of thumb is that there are usually more of these toxic nasties in dark-coloured drinks than in light, so brandy, whisky and red wine contain many more cogeners than gin, vodka and white wine, ergo it's the former group that generally cause the worst hangovers.

Alcohol is a diuretic, which causes dehydration through increased urination. Coffee is also a diuretic, so when you're suffering after an excessive night out, don't turn for the coffee pot, turn instead for good old water – and plenty of it, as soon as you can. Before you go to bed, drink a pint of water. When you get up in the morning, drink another pint. If you have a headache, take paracetamol rather than aspirin, as aspirin is more likely to irritate your already grumbling stomach.

And then again, there is the age-old cure … stay off the booze in the first place!

Grandfathers enjoy their time in the kitchen. It gives them an opportunity to be creative and to experiment. Food, along with plenty of exercise, plays an important part in keeping Grandfather fit and well. Eat healthily but at the same time remember – everything in moderation, 'A little bit of what you fancy does you good!'

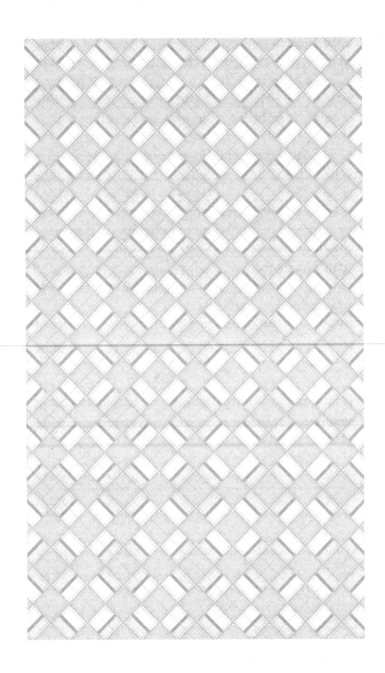

Looking Good and Feeling Fit

'You are old, Father William,' the young man said,
'And your hair has become very white;
And yet you incessantly stand on your head –
Do you think, at your age, it is right?'

Lewis Carroll (1832–1898)

Older people are often perceived as round-shouldered, grumpy, incapable old gits – and it's this negative stereotyping that has led to one of the few remaining discriminations still to be addressed – 'ageism'. But the truth is that most grandparents and older people do not recognize this perception of themselves and deplore the image. After all, you can be a grandparent pretty early on in life.

Even my wife, albeit light-heartedly, said, when we got the news we were going to be grandparents, that she looked forward to the prospect of becoming a grandma, but she wasn't so sure that she liked the idea of sleeping with a grandad!

It is always wonderful to hear of the many fantastic achievements of older people in the arts, sports, service to the community and other creative fields. Retirement opens the door to many opportunities that previously had been time-constrained, and becoming a grandfather brings with it a whole array of new experiences. You have the opportunity to pass on a lifetime of wisdom and knowledge that is valuable to younger people and offers links to the past, which gives a sense of continuity throughout the generations.

Tips for a top look

I'm no style guru myself, but if you want to look your best, my number one piece of advice is: put a big smile on your face. You don't have to go mad, but a bright, friendly, open demeanour will get you a long way in this world.

And there are a few other tips that might help:

- The shaggy look is for kids and teens, not older men.

- Likewise, ponytails are for young ladies (and a few younger men, I suppose). An old crusty with a greasy ponytail is a terrible sight.

- You don't have to be rich to look good. Make sure your clothes are presentable, that you are clean and tidy and get on out there!

Caring for your clothes

How to fix torn clothes

This all depends on the severity of the rip and where it is. When you need to mend 'important' items such as a dinner jacket you should really leave that to the professionals. However, smaller tears on shirts, trousers and jumpers are fairly easy to fix. One way is to use iron-on mending tape that you can buy in all good department stores.

- Buy the tape in the colour that's the best match for your garment – and make sure it's the washable type.
- Turn the torn garment inside out and cut the tape to the required length, adding an extra centimetre or so all the way round.
- Trim any straggly threads away from the torn edges and put the edges of the tear as flat and close together as possible.
- Iron the back of the torn area to help the edges meet cleanly.
- Lay the tape on the tear, adhesive side down and iron over it to bond the tape and the fabric.
- Leave the garment to cool.

You should have a fairly clean and neat mend. You can also use this tape to fix holes in trouser and coat pockets – you'll never lose your loose change again.

How to prevent moth holes in clothes

My mother's way to get rid of moths was with cedar wood. She would hang cedar wood balls in the wardrobe and put them in the chest of drawers and I always remember the very pleasant smell and thinking how odd it was that the moth didn't like it! The other thing she used was mothballs, but the smell can be pretty overpowering, so use these sparingly.

Nowadays we don't seem to be able to get rid of these pests easily, and you are more likely to keep moths at bay with cedar wood and mothballs than get rid of them. But there are a few things you can try to minimize the risk of getting the blasted things in the first place.

- ✻ Don't leave your clothes hanging in the wardrobe for months – air them regularly and if you have to leave them for any length of time, invest in vacuum-sealed plastic carriers so that moths can't get in.

✖ If you have fitted wardrobes, don't put carpet in them as they attract moths and act as a very comfortable breeding ground.

✖ Use a vacuum to clean your wardrobe – but be sure to empty the cleaner afterwards or else the larvae might just start growing again.

✖ Keep your clothes clean. Moths are attracted to the smell of human sweat.

✖ If you have moths, you might have to wash your clothes at a hotter temperature than you would usually. The larvae won't be killed off at a lower temperature.

Shoe care

How to shine shoes

Nowadays people buy those 'instant shine' foam shoe buffers that are said to be impregnated with shoe polish, and for a quick fix keeping one of those in your desk drawer can do the trick. But to get a proper shine that you can see your face in, there's nothing like a spit-shine to make that footwear gleam.

✖ Apply a layer of shoe polish all over the shoe and leave to dry for five minutes.

✄ Take a clean, soft cloth and wrap it around your index finger, then spit on the cloth and, using small circular movements, buff the dried polish with the cloth, and you'll see the wax in the polish take on a good shine.

✄ Work the polish in, then add another layer of polish onto the shoe and work that in with the cloth, repeating so that you build up an even shine.

✄ Take another soft, clean cloth and buff your shoes one final time.

How to re-sole shoes

Make sure you have bought a replacement sole of the correct type and size before you start ripping the old sole off your shoe. This fix is not meant for trainers, but rather for more formal lace-ups or slip-ons with a proper sole.

✄ Make sure the shoe is clean and dry, then take a craft knife and carefully cut the old sole away.

- Then take a piece of sandpaper and buff over the bottom of the shoe to remove any old glue and to give the surface a rough finish in order to grip the new sole when it's stuck on.
- Sand the surface of the new sole, giving it a rough finish which will help sole and shoe bond together.
- Check the manufacturer's instructions on the glue you are using. There are several shoe repair glues available (and some are quite toxic, so take care).
- Apply a good spread of the glue onto the base of the shoe and the new sole then align the two parts and press together firmly.
- It's best to leave the glue to reach maximum bond strength before wearing the shoe, so if you can, lightly clamp the shoe for twenty-four hours.
- If you need to, using your craft knife, trim any excess sole away from the shoe and buff with the sandpaper to get a good finish.

Sole clever

For a quick repair to a hole in the sole, take two lengths of waterproof duct tape and apply one to the inside and one to the outside of the sole – that should get you to the interview on time!

How to clean suede shoes

When the shoes are dry, scrape off any heavy mud, then, using a circular motion, brush the shoes with a suede brush made of bristle or wire. Gently sponge away any kick or scuff marks using a mild soap and water solution and remove any ingrained dirt with a suede shampoo, following the manufacturer's instructions. Take care to avoid flattening the nap of the suede.

Cleaning fabric shoes

Some fabric shoes can be placed in a pillowcase and machine-washed, but for more formal fabric shoes, brush off any heavy dirt when the shoes are dry and apply a fabric cleaner of a suitable colour to keep them in good condition.

Storing shoes

Shoe or boot trees are very useful for keeping the items in shape, and if you have the space, store them in boxes to avoid further scuffs and keep out dust. Try to avoid wearing the same shoes day after day, they will last longer and keep their shape better if you rest them occasionally.

Clear nail varnish

I bet you never thought you'd hear Grandad talk about this stuff, but clear nail varnish is an absolute must for any repairman's toolbox.

✖ A ladder in your tights, Grandma? Dab a spot of this stuff on, that'll stop it running any further.

✖ Keep losing buttons on that jacket? Apply a spot of clear nail varnish onto the thread and those buttons will be secure forever.

✖ A little scuff or dent in a polished wood floor? Touch it up with a drop of clear nail varnish.

✖ Fed up of the ends of your shoelaces unravelling? Dip them in clear nail varnish.

Keep going, Grandad!

To get full enjoyment out of being both a grandfather and an older person, you have to keep fit, mentally and physically. The brain and the body need to remain active. Even Plato (born *c.* 427 BC) recognized the importance of the inter-relationships of the functions of body and the mind for harmonious well-being.

My dictum for a healthy old age – *any* age – is 'Eat well, keep moving and challenge the brain'.

Eat well

✳ Making sure you eat at least five portions of fruit or vegetables a day has become a useful goal. Even children know the beneficial effects of fruit and vegetables, the only problem is making sure they eat them.

✳ Reducing the intake of saturated fats, sugar and salt that often feature in ready-prepared meals is important for a healthy diet, so it is worthwhile to read the labels.

✳ Drinking plenty of fluids, especially water – two litres a day is recommended to prevent dehydration.

✳ Obesity is a real problem in many countries. Being overweight can be a result of a sedentary lifestyle and an unhealthy diet. It not only reduces mobility but also increases the risk of diabetes and cardiac problems – eat to live, don't live to eat.

✳ Snacking in the evening can be quite a problem. If you have been active all day you can perhaps treat yourself to a couple of pieces of chocolate with your coffee, but if you still feel like nibbling, then go to the fruit bowl.

Keep moving

Keeping physically fit and active contributes to the enjoyment of the retirement years and is essential if you are a grandfather and want to play an active role with your grandchildren. There are many different ways of keeping fit – you don't have to join a gym to stay agile. The benefit of regular exercise is that it reduces health risks by helping to:

- keep arteries healthy

- reduce anxiety

- lower blood pressure

- stimulate blood vessels

- improve balance and prevent falls

- help speed up recovery time

- improve strength and muscle tone

- improve mobility, flexibility and endurance

- produce the feel-good factor

- help with cognitive abilities

- help to improve the quality of life

- improve bone density

✂ increase energy levels

✂ improve sleep

How to start an exercise programme

If you have not been active for some time, it is advisable to have a medical check-up and discuss with your doctor the sort of fitness programme you want to follow. If you're thinking of joining a fitness centre they will carry out an assessment and ask you questions about your medical history before designing a personal programme to suit your needs.

While any exercise is better than none at all, aiming to be more active more often is the way to start. Make sure you start slowly and build up your level of activity. Don't overdo it by exercising to exhaustion and certainly do not exercise if you feel unwell.

Deep breathing

Deep-breathing exercises are easy to do and effective in promoting relaxation, refreshing the cells of the body, lowering blood pressure and assisting with the removal of toxins. The relaxation helps to ease headaches and can be beneficial for asthma sufferers. When I was young it was considered healthy and rather macho to start the day by throwing open the bedroom window, whatever the weather, and taking deep breaths of the cool morning air.

These days I practise deep breathing by relaxing in a chair, away from any diversions, breathing in through the nose deeply, holding for a moment and then slowly exhaling through the mouth. I aim to manage eight to ten breaths a minute. Deep-breathing exercises can be done at any time of the day and are best if done on a regular basis, three to four times a week. I find this simple exercise effective and I do it for ten minutes a session. It certainly helps to keep my blood pressure in check.

Get walking

This is probably the most common form of activity and, if done briskly, is a good aerobic (relating to the health of the heart and lungs) form of movement that enables the red blood cells to pass oxygen around the body more efficiently, resulting in the heart being under less strain.

You can help maintain a good level of fitness by taking a brisk walk, lasting about twenty minutes, three times a week. Start slowly if you are unfit and always work within your level of ability. If you are walking alone, why not do some stretching activities while you walk? Swing your arms just that little bit more; do some deep breathing; lengthen your stride a little so that you can feel a slight stretch in your thighs.

When walking avoid stooping, something that can easily happen if the head is allowed to jut forward when carrying a backpack. Keep the rucksack close to your body, not loose or sagging down, and stretch upwards with your shoulders back – 'think tall'.

Don't overdo it, but enjoy the feeling – in the knowledge that you can relax with a smug grin of satisfaction when you get home.

Exercising at home – flexibility

To keep your body trim and flexible it is necessary to prevent spinal and other muscles from becoming shortened and stiff, hence the following general stretching exercises. All these exercises can be done at home, and some grandfathers will recognize the activities from their PT or PE lessons at school – and may now appreciate their value, even if they didn't at the time.

Shoulders

- Stand with one leg forward and bent at the knee, with the same side hand resting on the knee. Swing the opposite arm in circles, brushing the ear and as close to the body as possible, five times forward and five times backwards. Repeat on the opposite side.

- Stand or sit with hands in front of chest and elbows held in line with the shoulders pointing outwards. Pull the elbows back on each count of one, two, then return. Repeat.

- Instead of pulling elbows back, circle them first one way then the other.

Waist

- Stand with feet shoulder-width apart and legs straight or sit in an armless chair. Lean over, stretching to the right, the hand brushing the knee if standing, or past the chair side if sitting. Repeat to the left. Increase repetitions with practice.
- Standing, link thumbs and draw a circle as big as possible round the head. Repeat the other way.
- Standing or sitting, raise the arms as far as possible above the head then bend at the waist to one side then the other. Repeat.

Neck

- Stand with feet apart and hands by your side, or sit in a comfortable but firm chair. Look ahead then turn the head slowly to the right and back again, then repeat to the left. Repeat each movement up to ten times.
- Use the same starting position and slowly move the chin down to the chest, followed by tilting the head back. Repeat up to ten times. If you feel any discomfort, stop the exercise.

Legs

- Balance on one leg or, for support, hold on to a chair back or the wall with one hand and swing the opposite leg forward and backward.

- Follow on by lifting leg to the side and returning and then to the back and returning. Repeat on the other side.

- Place one leg in front of the other, with relaxed knees and trunk upright, gently bounce up and down bending both knees.

Exercising at home – strength

As well as flexibility, it is important to strengthen the muscles – particularly useful for keeping up with the grandkids on the football pitch!

Arm, leg and ankle

- Stand erect, lifting heels off the floor and at the same time breathing in and raising both arms forward to shoulder level. Hold for a moment before exhaling as the heels and arms are lowered. Lower the arms as if pushing down an imaginary weight. Repeat ten times.

- Without using the arms, lift toes and heels alternately.

- Lifting alternate legs off the ground, circle the ankle to the left and to the right.

- Using the back of a chair for support if necessary, bend the knees slightly and bounce twice, then stand up. Gradually increase the amount the knees bend. If possible, link fingers, palms facing outwards and push arms forward as you bend.

- Stand close to a tabletop, place the hands on the edge, bend at the elbows until body is close to the table and push back by straightening the arms. The resistance can be increased by gradually placing the hands on something lower until on the floor (a press-up). To increase the load further still, start to raise the legs by placing them on something above ground level.

- Sitting in a chair or lying down, lift the legs, hold, then return to rest. Try raising the legs to different heights and try a cycling motion.

Posture

In the old days we were always told to 'keep the shoulders back and walk as if balancing a book on our head'. Generations earlier, high-backed wooden chairs were made to encourage children to have good sitting postures. Attention to good carriage seems to have declined over recent years.

The benefits of good posture

- Looks attractive and both gives and shows a feeling of confidence.
- Muscles can be used more efficiently since joints and bones are in correct alignment.
- The lungs can work more efficiently.
- Reduces the wear and tear on joints, which can cause arthritis.
- Helps maintain the normal curvature of the spine.
- Helps to prevent backache.

The longer poor posture continues, the more difficult it is to correct it. Older people can form bad postural habits by letting their head jut forward and their shoulders sag.

To effect good posture, which should be second nature, align the ears, shoulders, hips and ankles to make a straight line, so that the normal curvature of the spine is maintained.

Sitting posture

Aim to:

❋ Place buttocks so that they touch the back of the chair.

❋ Sit up straight.

❋ Place a cushion or similar in the small of the back.

❋ After sitting for an hour (at the most), stand up and move around before sitting down again.

❋ When standing up, move to the edge of the chair/settee and stand by using the legs. Avoid bending forward from the waist to stand up.

Lifting posture

Always avoid lifting anything too heavy, but when lifting things from the floor make sure that you:

❋ Stand with your feet apart.

❋ Stand close to the object you are picking up.

❋ Crouch down, bending your knees and using your leg and stomach muscles for lifting, not the lower back.

❋ Lift smoothly.

❋ Do not bend down from the waist.

Grumpy no more!

Remember, whatever your age, faulty posture throws added strain on muscles and joints that can lead to problems as you age, so it's well worth bearing all these exercises in mind throughout life.

So, even though Grandfather's hair may be white like Old Father William's (he may not choose to stand on his head), following the advice of 'Eat Well, Keep Moving and Challenge the Brain' he has a good chance of remaining fit and healthy into old age and dispelling the image of a round-shouldered, grumpy old git.

Grandfather Indoors

By the time you become a grandfather, chances are that you'll be settled in a house that you have worked hard to buy, maintain and fill with all the memories of a fruitful life. But when it comes to taking pride in one's home, you don't have to spend a fortune. Many traditional cleaning methods cannot be beaten, and as for DIY tips, Grandad's your man!

Some tips for general maintenance

✄ File all appliance instruction manuals and guarantees for easy reference.

✄ Make sure that any equipment that requires servicing is done regularly, including the chimney being swept.

✄ Install and regularly check smoke alarms.

✖ Check the lagging on vulnerable pipes and taps, especially in the garage, garden shed or outside.

✖ Dripping taps – turn off water at the mains and replace the washer. Remember to put the plug in the sink to avoid losing any bits down the plughole (very frustrating!)

✖ Unblock troublesome drains.

✖ Catch up on all those little problems waiting to be fixed!

Cleaning the traditional way

The first thing to do to make cleaning easier is to ensure you have all your 'equipment' together in one place. Fill a box or basket with all the essential cleaning products – polish, dusters, bleach, scrubbing brush etc. and cart it around as you

go. There's nothing worse than having to stop and go back to the kitchen cupboard to find something. Once you've decided to clean – get on with it!

There are a few cleaning essentials that it's worth having around all the time – and they aren't what you might expect!

Dear old vinegar

You only have to look at what happens if you soak a grimy penny in a bowl of white distilled vinegar to see that it's a great cleaning agent. Over the years, I've used it on many jobs around the house and beyond – from cleaning the showerhead to deodorizing the car. A half-and-half solution of clear vinegar and water will clean most worktops and kitchen gadgets (but you must never use it on marble, as it might damage a marble surface). It's cheap and environmentally friendly too, so everybody wins. So, apart from its culinary uses, here are some of the best ways to use vinegar.

- ✂ Getting rid of limescale – To de-scale a kettle, fill the kettle with half water and half white distilled vinegar, put it on to boil and leave the mixture in the kettle to cool overnight. Next morning, before using it, make sure you refill the kettle with fresh water and boil several times, using clean water every time.

- ✂ Cleaning windows – Vinegar is fantastic for cleaning glass. Add white distilled vinegar to your water, clean, then wipe dry with a cloth. For a really sparkling shine, finish with a sheet of screwed-up newspaper.

- Chrome – always a tricky one, clean your sink top or other chrome surface with a paste of two tablespoons of salt mixed with one tablespoon of white distilled vinegar. To clean chrome taps, soak a piece of cloth in white distilled vinegar and wrap it around the tap. Leave it overnight and wipe sparkling clean in the morning.

- Cleaning the grill – you can make life easier by preparing the grill pan for cleaning by spraying on a solution of half water, half white distilled vinegar. This lifts the burnt-on stains and makes them easier to wipe away. You can also use vinegar to clean the glass oven door. If there are stains that need attention, spray on undiluted vinegar and leave for ten minutes before wiping away with a cloth.

- Cleaning the dishwasher – to get rid of odours and keep the dishwasher in sparkling condition, pour a cup of white distilled vinegar inside the empty machine and run it through a whole cycle.

- Refrigerator – wipe your fridge door seals with white vinegar every now and then to keep them free of mould.

- Thermos flasks – if you just can't get that lingering smell out of your thermos, add a couple of tablespoons of vinegar to the flask and top up with hot water. Leave the mixture for half an hour then pour it away and rinse thoroughly – job done.

✽ Glasses – for extra sparkle in your glassware, add a good splash of vinegar to your hot (but not boiling) soapy water when cleaning them.

Bicarbonate of soda

Similar to vinegar in its multi-uses, bicarb (or baking soda) is a useful ingredient for your household cupboard. It is fantastic at absorbing nasty smells and can be a very useful cleaning agent – again, it's cheap and environmentally friendly.

✽ For lingering odours on soft furnishings, sprinkle on and leave for three to four hours before vacuuming off.

✽ To get rid of odours inside the fridge or microwave place a bowl of bicarbonate on a shelf and leave to stand overnight. (You can actually leave the bowl of soda in the fridge or freezer and simply stir it every now and again so that it keeps absorbing odours. Change it every month or so and you'll have an odour-free appliance.)

✽ When washing the inside of the fridge or freezer use bicarbonate of soda dissolved in warm water to leave it clean and fresh smelling.

✽ Bicarb can also be used as a cleaner for stubborn marks by mixing it with water to make a paste and spreading on delicate plastic surfaces such as a fridge or freezer.

That smells nice!

This is a great tip for a fragrant room. Put a few drops of Grandma's favourite perfume or your favourite after-shave on a cold lightbulb (when the light is off, of course). When you turn the light on, the heat produced will activate the essence of the perfume and the scent will fill the room.

Lemon juice

A very satisfactory bleach and disinfectant, as well as having a wonderful fragrance, a single lemon can go a long way.

✂ Half a lemon can be used to clean the hands after doing messy household jobs.

✂ Using the other half, sprinkle with salt and rub on brass or copper, rinse off and polish dry for a bright shine.

✂ Use lemon in a microwave to get rid of dried-on bits of food – simply put four slices in a bowl of hot water and set the microwave on high for about seven minutes, then wipe the inside of the microwave.

Chopping boards

To stop a wooden chopping board from splitting, rub it with a little vegetable oil every now and then. To get rid of food odours, rub the board with salt and half a lemon.

Cleaning tarnished metal

Another of those jobs that, though messy, gives me a warm glow of satisfaction every time!

Silver

Bicarbonate of soda and aluminium foil is a great way to clean silver. Whether you have a big item such as a teapot or you want to shine up your jewellery, try this easy fix (there is some chemical reason why this works but I can't remember it!).

- ❃ Take a heatproof dish that's large enough to fully submerge your item and place a piece of aluminium foil, shiny side up, on the bottom.

- ❃ Put the item on the foil and sprinkle over bicarbonate of soda.

- ❃ Pour a kettle of boiling water over the item and watch the tarnish on your silver float off onto the foil.

Gold

Submerge the gold item in hot soapy water (use washing-up liquid) for about fifteen minutes then scrub it gently with an old, soft toothbrush. Rinse in lukewarm water then shine with a soft cloth. For stubborn stains, add a little white toothpaste (gel toothpaste doesn't work) and work it in with the toothbrush. Wash it off and buff to a shine with a soft cloth.

Brass

From candlesticks to fireplace tools, brass is a lovely metal to have around the home – but it takes some cleaning! Or does it? These natural tips all work a treat and will save you the money of buying proprietary brands.

- Often, brass will come up nicely with a simple wash in warm soapy water. Make sure you dry the item well after washing and buff it up to a good shine.

- Good old lemon juice and salt cleans brass very effectively. Cut a lemon in half then spread table salt over the cut edge and rub the salt-coated lemon on the brass, recoating the lemon with salt as necessary. Then buff the brass with a clean dry cloth.

- Rub plain yoghurt into the brass and leave to dry, then use a clean dry cloth to buff up the shine.

My metal saucepan's gone rusty

This works for any rusty pans or baking trays. Cut a raw potato in half, sprinkle it with washing powder and, using it like a scouring pad, scrub the pan with it. Somehow the starch from the potato and the cleaning agents in the detergent combine to power through the rust and bring the metalware back into good condition. Magic.

Keeping and repairing china

The best way to keep china in good shape is to make sure you clean and store it correctly in the first place.

- Fine china – especially hand-painted – should always be washed separately from other dishes and cutlery, using hot but not boiling water and using a non-abrasive cleaner. It should be rinsed immediately after use so that stains have no chance to latch on, and never ever put into a dishwasher.

- To store china cups, lay them on their sides in groups of four, with the handle of each cup inside the bowl of another, and place the group on stacked saucers.

- To prevent precious plates from chipping, put paper towels between them when stacking.

- Do not put hot food on cold plates (for the good of the food as well as the plate).

When breakages occur

If you break your favourite vase, try to mend it using a slow-setting epoxy glue. This glue is waterproof when set, and it also gives you time to adjust and reposition the pieces as necessary before it hardens.

- Clean the broken edges and mix the glue according to the manufacturer's instructions.

- Apply a thin coat of glue to both edges and press together.

- To make a really good join, bind the vase with adhesive tape so that an even and constant pressure is applied, and leave for at least twelve hours.

- Chip away any excess glue before it hardens completely.

Unfortunately, china that has been broken will never be as strong as it once was, so use your mended piece with caution. And if your broken china is of great sentimental value, do think about taking it to a professional restorer.

Quick china tips

- To remove hairline cracks in piece of china, soak it overnight in a bowl of warm milk. In the morning, wash it gently and you should find the tiny cracks have disappeared.
- To remove stubborn stains on the insides of tea and coffee cups, put a little bicarbonate of soda on a damp cloth and scrub the offending stain.

Decluttering

There's a wise old Chinese proverb that says, 'It is not the furniture in a room that makes it habitable but the space.' We are all guilty of building up clutter, keeping things that we think one day might come in handy. But taking control of your possessions and thinking through what you truly value can be a cathartic exercise.

One thing that really annoys me is when I find that I have more than one of the same item. I'm always buying screwdrivers, for example. Why? Not because I need a different size – oh no. Because I've forgotten where I put the first one (or Grandma has lost it). If you look at it this way, by decluttering you could sort your life out and save money!

Make a start

The easiest way to start decluttering is to get yourself three large cardboard boxes and mark them thus:

- ✱ Throw away (or recycle) – for good old junk that you know should go out.

- ✱ Give away – for the things that you know you won't use or wear ever again but could still have some value to others.

- ✱ Keep – for the things that you know you want but that need to be stowed away somewhere rather than dumped in full view in your living room.

Look around your house, room by room, pick up an object and ask yourself three simple questions:

- ✱ Will I ever use it again?

- ✱ Have I even looked at it lately?

- ✱ Is this something I would grab if the house was on fire?

I know it's often not quite as straightforward as that, but this is a starting point. As your three boxes fill up with items you might just notice a lightening of the heart – not to mention all that space!

A place for everything and everything in its place

Go through your house room by room and organize your life.

THE LIVING ROOM

- Try to avoid having too many ornaments and knick-knacks, they only mean more dusting.

- Get some racks for CDs and DVDs – and make it a rule that whoever is watching the film, playing the game or listening to music puts said item away when finished!

- Sort through newspapers and magazines regularly and recycle as necessary – don't let them pile up.

- Mail – Don't pile it up, file it away! Get yourself a concertina file or a few ordinary folders and label them usefully – 'car', 'insurance', 'bank', tax' etc. Fill the file up as the material comes in the mail. This way at least you know where everything is when you come to need it, rather than being faced with searching through a toppling tower of paper. Junk mail goes straight into the recycling bin.

THE KITCHEN

- Keep appliances you don't use every day, such as blenders or food processors, hidden away in a cupboard so that you can keep your work surfaces clear and tidy.

- Organize your cupboards so that you have easy access to the things you use most, and recycle the items you have never used (we all have some of these).

- Sort out your ingredients and throw out anything past its sell-by date.

THE BEDROOM

- Get right to the back of your wardrobe or chest of drawers to find all those old clothes that you haven't worn for years. Are you going to wear them ever again? Do they still fit? Are they of value to anyone else? Answer, throw away or give away.

- For the rest, buy a couple of transparent plastic storage boxes to keep your out-of-season clothes in. They come in many sizes and with lids that seal to keep moths out.

- Sort your shoes out – yes, attack that tangled mess at the bottom of your wardrobe by making (or buying) a shelving rack for your shoes. Throw out the ones beyond repair and any you haven't actually got around to wearing (even though you've had them for years).

THE BATHROOM

- Think about what you really need in this room and clear out all unnecessary items.

✁ Ask Grandma to sort out her make-up and perfume (and you sort through your grooming products) and get rid of any old or unwanted pieces, then make sure there is somewhere to store any remaining.

✁ Make sure to use all the wall space you need for extra storage, especially in smaller bathrooms. Thin shelves over the toilet cistern can hold a huge array of bathroom necessities and keep them out of the way.

How to fix a creaking door

With inside doors, it's not usually the door that creaks, but the hinges, and the creaking generally occurs when there's not enough lubricant on the hinge or the hinge pin (inside the hinge), resulting in friction. A squirt of light lubricant such as WD40 should do the trick in most cases.

For an outside wooden door, these are more prone to swelling and contracting as a result of the weather. Have a look at the hinge screws and make sure they are tightened down and make sure there is no dirt in the hinges or around the doorjamb. If absolutely necessary, take the door off its hinges and shave it down with a wood plane – not the easiest fix to do, but always effective.

Top drilling tip

When you want to drill into the ceiling, make a hole in the bottom of a shop-bought round aluminium flan tray and put the drill bit through that … the tray will catch the dust and your eyes will be dust-free.

How to fix a sticking lock

You might be tempted to squirt a little WD40 or other lubricant into a sticking lock, but beware, that could eventually make the problem worse, as any greasy substance will attract dirt, which will build up more and more … and cause the lock to stick again.

The best thing to use is graphite powder, available in good hardware stores, and puff a little graphite through the container nozzle into the lock. Don't use too much, a little will do the job. Test the lock and add a little more graphite as necessary. If you find you have to repeat this job on the same lock again and again, it might be time to change the lock!

Quick fixes

✂ Is your metal bed frame squeaking? Dab a little baby powder on the joints for a better night's sleep.

✂ Creaking floorboards? Sprinkle a little talcum powder on the offending boards, step on them a few times to work the powder in and brush off the excess.

How to build a fire

I don't know about you, but it's always been my job to build the fire and clean it out the next day. It seems to be a 'dad job', but I've realized that now many dads (and mums) don't actually know how to build an efficient fire in the fireplace and how to keep it going well.

First things first

Of course, the first thing to check is that your chimney is clean. A rule of thumb is to have your chimney swept at least once a year, depending on what you can burn in your local area. A good chimney sweep will ensure that no blockages occur and reduce the risk of nasty fumes building up.

Before you start, make sure the fireplace is thoroughly cleaned out and no ash from the previous fire remains. If you have a flue, make sure it is open.

It's all in the wood

When you have selected your wood, make sure some of it is cut into thin strips about 10 inches long by 2 inches thick to use for kindling. Scrunch up about five sheets of newspaper for tinder, and place them in the fireplace, then lay the kindling sticks on top of the newspaper and a couple of smallish logs on top of the kindling.

Next, take a match or firelighter and light a couple of pieces of the newspaper, one at one side of the fire, the other opposite it, so that the newspaper will start it off, lighting the kindling first before progressing on to the logs a few minutes later.

Burn, baby, burn!

As the logs begin to burn, add more, stacking them on top of the pile. If you are using coal, add a few pieces at a time, but remember that in order to burn effectively your fire needs oxygen to circulate freely around all the logs (and coal) as they burn, so don't add too much at once.

Use a poker to adjust your wood and coal. We used to use bellows when I was a lad (another way of encouraging the fire), but I don't expect you can find these so readily now.

And when it's burned out, you can put the ash on the compost heap.

A word about wood

Always make sure your wood is dry. Care is needed in choosing the wood. The logs should be seasoned before they are burned, ideally storing them for at least two years after they were cut. It is useful to stock up in the spring for use the following winter. See page 129 for how to make a log store.

Logs to burn

This traditional English folk poem is a useful guide to buying or cutting wood.

> Logs to burn, logs to burn;
> Logs to save the coal a turn.
>
> Here's a word to make you wise
> When you hear the woodman's cries;
> Never heed his usual tale
> That he has splendid logs for sale
> But read these lines and really learn,
> The proper kind of logs to burn.
>
> OAK logs will warm you well,
> If they're old and dry.
> LARCH logs of pinewoods smell
> But the sparks will fly.
> BEECH logs for Christmas time;
> YEW logs heat well;
> SCOTCH logs it is a crime

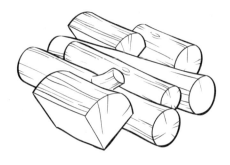

For anyone to sell.
BIRCH logs will burn too fast;
CHESTNUT scarce at all;
HAWTHORNE logs are good to last
If cut in the fall.
HOLLY logs will burn like wax,
You should burn them green;
ELM logs like smouldering flax,
No flame to be seen.
PEAR logs and APPLE logs,
They will scent your room;
CHERRY logs across the dogs
Smell like flowers in bloom,
But ASH logs, all smooth and grey
Burn them green or old,
Buy up all that come your way,
They're worth their weight in gold.

Washday

Traditionally washday was always on a Monday and usually took most of the day. It involved boiling, scrubbing on the washboard (which was also used as a musical instrument in skiffle and country and western bands), agitating the clothes to clean and rinse by twisting and turning the dolly pegs in the dolly tub, then turning the heavy handle of the mangle to squeeze out the water as the clothes went through the rollers – being careful to keep your fingers out of the way.

The washing was hung out to dry in the wind and sunshine when possible. There's nothing like a blow in the sun to lift tired-looking white fabrics. Hang tea towels, sheets and white hankies out in the sunshine if you can – they'll smell fresher than any tumble dryer can make them and with any luck the sun will help to bleach out stubborn stains.

Helpful laundry hints

- ❋ Always sort the clothes into piles, e.g. whites, coloureds and darks, following laundry instructions.

- ❋ For economy always try to wait until you have a full load.

- ❋ When possible, hang the clothes out to dry. Not only will you save the cost of drying them in your tumble dryer but they will also feel softer, smell fresher and be much easier to iron, and some may not need ironing at all.

✖ Before you hang your washing out, make sure your pegs are free from rust and that the washing line is clean.

✖ Clothes are much easier to iron if they are folded when they are brought from the line, particularly sheets. It's useful to enlist help when folding sheets (I've been enlisted many times over the years, which is why I know all about it).

✖ Any clothes that are 100 per cent cotton will always iron better if they are damped, rolled up and left for a while before ironing.

✖ Some fabrics – such as linen – are better ironed on the wrong side to prevent shining or ironed under a damp cloth

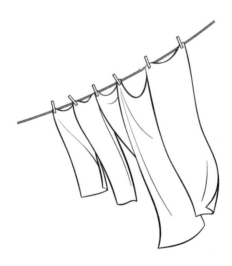

- Put a sheet of aluminium foil under your ironing board cover – it will reflect the heat and also save energy.

- When ironing embroidered articles do a final press on the wrong side to make the embroidery stand out.

Some age-old remedies

There are a number of remedies I remember my mother using in my childhood, which had in turn been passed down to her, that are still used effectively today.

Blackberry vinegar

When diluted with hot water this delicious drink is soothing for sore throats, colds and coughs. I always add a tot of whisky or rum when taking at bedtime. This recipe was written down several generations ago – and is looking very faded after so many years. It is the recipe we still use at home today.

- Pour 1 litre (2 pints) of pure malt vinegar over 3 quarts of ripe blackberries.

- Cover and leave for at least 24 hours (I leave it for several days).

- Bruise the fruit and strain the mixture.

- To every litre of juice add 900 g (2 lb) of sugar, then boil the mixture gently for 20 minutes, leave to cool and bottle. The vinegar should keep well for at least a year. Use a small quantity with cold or hot water according to taste (it is also delicious used undiluted on pancakes).

Elderberry syrup

Diluted with hot water, this makes another soothing drink for when suffering from a cold.

✂ Collect bunches of elderberries and, using a fork, remove the berries from the stalks.

✂ Put the berries in a pan and cover with water. Bring to a boil and simmer for 20 minutes.

✂ Strain the liquid, and to each 56 ml (1 pint) juice add 1 lb sugar, 10 cloves and 2 cinnamon sticks (broken up). Boil for 10 minutes.

✂ Cool, then bottle in sterilized bottles dividing the cinnamon and cloves between the bottles.

✂ The syrup should keep for up to a year.

Rosehip syrup

Health professionals used to routinely prescribe rosehip syrup for children because of the high vitamin C content. Should you find rosehips in the hedgerows, please note that they should not be picked until after the first frost, when their vitamin content is at its highest. The hips should be fresh, deep red and fully ripe.

�֎ Crush or grate the berries and put into boiling water, allowing 1.7 l (3 pints) water to 900 g (2 lb) fruit.

✷ Bring to boil again and set aside for 10 minutes, then strain the liquid through a jelly bag until it ceases to drip and set the juice to one side.

✷ Return the pulp from the bag to the pan and add a further 85 ml (1½ pints) boiling water. Bring to the boil and leave for 10 minutes, then strain as before.

✷ Mix the two juices and boil until the combined juice is reduced to about 85 ml (1½ pints). Add 450g (1 lb) sugar and stir until dissolved.

✷ Bottle the syrup and keep in a cool cupboard.

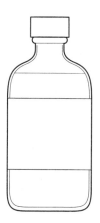

Other tried and tested soothers for coughs, colds and sore throats

�֍ Swede juice – helps to relieve a persistent cough. Peel and cube a small swede and liberally sprinkle with sugar to draw out the juice. Cover with a plate and leave for several hours. The resulting thick, sweet syrup taken slowly from a spoon helps to stop the irritation in the throat.

✖ Lemon and honey – a classic soother. Cut up a lemon and cover with about a pint of almost boiling water. Mix in plenty of honey and stir well, crushing the lemon against the side of the jug. Cover and leave to infuse (soothing when hot, refreshing when cold).

✖ Warm milk and honey acts in the same way.

✖ Butter, sugar and vinegar mixed together in a cup and taken a little at a time from a spoon has stopped many a night-time cough.

Other ailments

✖ Chewing a clove or dabbing oil of cloves on the affected tooth can give temporary relief from toothache.

✖ Ground ginger stirred into hot water can relieve travel sickness and an upset tummy.

- Tisanes or herbal infusions have been used through the generations for their medicinal properties and many of the common ingredients required can be found in our fields and hedgerows. They can be drunk either hot or cold, adding honey to taste. For a pick-me-up use fresh or dried nettles or rosehips and roses. Elderflowers and berries can be used to calm the nerves and reduce sleeplessness.

The Great Outdoors

'To forget how to dig the earth and tend to the soil is to forget ourselves.'

MAHATMA GANDHI

I'm not going to give you an A–Z of 'how to garden' in this chapter, rather I want to impart some old advice and the experience I've gleaned over the years working in my own garden and from family, friends and colleagues. Working in the garden serves a dual purpose, providing both exercise and pleasure. The fruits of your labour are there for all to see and enjoy, no matter how big or small the garden. There is something wonderfully fulfilling about sitting in a garden that you have created, on a summer's day, sharing it with family or friends, listening to the drone of the bees and the singing of the birds, or even alone with a good book and a glass of wine.

Preparing the garden can be hard work, but the rewards can be tremendous – whether your garden is large or small, a patio or balcony, even a windowsill, they can all yield produce in the form of flowers, fruit, herbs and vegetables.

The windowsill garden

If you are fortunate enough to have a large inside kitchen windowsill, you can use it like a mini greenhouse, a good place to grow seedlings for planting out in the garden later. Depending on the space you have, it is possible to start off French beans, runner beans, courgettes, squashes, tomatoes, peppers and sweetcorn. And if you have nowhere to transplant your plants outside, there are plants that thrive to maturity on the windowsill.

- Cress, for example, can be easily sown on a bed of damp cotton wool or a damp paper towel placed in the bottom of a small margarine container. It will need watering every day, but there's nothing nicer than fresh cress on a salad.

- Salad leaves are fantastic in a pot on the windowsill. Again, they need daily watering but the results are terrific, and harvesting a few leaves from each plant to add a bit of colour to your salad brings a smile to the face every time. Try to vary the leaves you plant – rocket, watercress, spinach, chard, they all have distinctive flavours that will spice up any sandwich.

- Herbs will thrive on the kitchen windowsill. Select herbs that don't grow too tall or too wide – basil, parsley, chives, thyme, mint to name a few. Some can be grown from seed and others can be purchased already potted. Cutting them fresh as you need them encourages new growth and if looked after will keep you in supply for weeks.

The patio or balcony garden

A small patio or balcony can be planted intensively by simply taking advantage of walls and other vertical surfaces along with different levels of planting. This can result in an individual and productive garden – and you'll still find the time to sit and enjoy it.

Many plants – flowers, shrubs, vegetables, soft fruit, tomatoes and small trees – including fruit trees – can be successfully planted in small spaces. The most suitable vegetables for containers are compact and quick maturing plants like beetroot, peppers, dwarf beans and aubergines, and, of course, salad leaves. To give height to the garden, runner beans can be grown up cane wigwams, which will add colourful interest when in flower, attract the bees, and provide you with delicious beans. Tomato plants can be grown against a wall, while strawberries and herbs can be grown in strawberry pots.

Colour, aroma and taste!

Interspersed between the fruit and vegetables, try some sweet peas planted up a trellis to provide a beautiful array of colour and a pleasant aroma. The more you pick them the more they will grow. Nip off any pods that form and the plants will keep producing flowers all summer long.

What about some edible flowers? If your outdoor space is only small, try growing some pot marigolds, cowslips, borage, violets and lavender. All these flowers are delicious when picked, washed and sprinkled on a salad. Make sure you know what you are planting (some flowers are poisonous) and if you are gardening with children, make sure they understand that you can't just pick any old flower head and eat it.

To add variety and interest to the patio garden you can buy lots of pots in different sizes and colours, but be inventive and make some more unusual receptacles by recycling interesting household goods such as an old teapot, kitchen sink, buckets and so on (remember to make holes for drainage).

Watering balcony or patio pots

If your balcony or patio gets bright sunlight for long periods of the day, make sure you water your pots at a cooler time – preferably in the evening after the sun has gone down. If you find your plants have wilted in the sun, don't water them immediately, try to provide some shade for them to cool in then water them – it's less stressful for the plant.

A word about watering

In these days of dry summers it's important to make sure you water your garden in the most efficient way, conserving every precious drop of water while still giving your plants the maximum benefit. Here are a few tips on getting the most from your water.

- ✂ Depending on your garden's size, make sure you have at least one water butt to collect every drop of rain.

- ✂ Think about which plants need the water most and give them a good soak rather than a quick sprinkle.

- ✂ Cut your plants back where you can, so that the water is going to where the plant needs its energy – into making its flowers or producing vegetables, for example.

- ✂ Use mulch (compost, bark or gravel) around your plants to help conserve the water and prevent it from evaporating.

- ✂ Use your compost (see page 114) and dig it in well to improve the soil structure.

- ✂ If your lawn goes brown, I know it's a shame, but short of wasting water on a grand scale there's little you can do. Don't worry, though, it'll come back with the autumn rains.

Composting

If you can make room in your garden, a compost heap is a great addition and will serve you well with natural fertilizer that will improve the texture of the soil and boost levels of friendly bacteria, thus producing better crops. Making your own compost is free, easy and at the same time gets rid of a lot of your household and garden waste. You can either construct a wooden slatted composting bin or buy a plastic one.

Wood or plastic?

The advantages of a slatted wooden composting bin are:

- It is easier to manage.
- It can easily be forked over to speed up the composting process.
- It will keep the compost well aerated.
- It can be home-made to suit your requirements.

The advantages of a plastic composting bin are:

- It is convenient and movable.
- It conserves moisture and reduces the need to water.
- It has a tight fitting-lid that keeps in the warmth, so aiding the rotting process.

Both types of composting bins will take vegetable matter, garden green waste including weeds (but avoid pernicious weeds and weeds with seed heads) and grass cuttings. It also takes leaves, small twigs (shredded), scrunched-up paper, coffee grounds, tea bags, scrunched-up egg boxes and eggshells. Meat, cooked food and other food should definitely not go in as they can encourage vermin.

Making the fertilizer

Loosen the soil beneath the bin to help drainage and to help worms and bacteria to enter the bin. It is better to start composting using manure as a first layer and then adding more manure as the compost heap grows, to aid the decomposition process. Compost heaps need moisture, green materials for nitrogen, brown material for carbon and air. Cold ash from a log fire also adds carbon. Eggshells add useful minerals. You need to keep the greens and the browns balanced. If the compost is too wet, add more browns; if too dry, add more greens. The contents should be mixed and turned over to add air, and watering is occasionally needed if the compost gets too dry.

Make your own wormery

If space is an issue in your garden, why not turn to the gardeners' best friend and create your own wormery. These compact wonders are fantastic for smaller gardens, and do the same job as a compost heap – but in less than half the space. All you need are the following items:

- A small plastic bin or box with a lid

✂ A plastic tap (e.g. a water butt tap)

✂ A 20 cm (8 in.) square piece of wire mesh

✂ Sand or gravel

✂ Some small pieces of wood

✂ Shredded newspaper or straw

✂ Composting worms (not the same as garden worms, but widely available)

Drill a hole in the bin or box about 5 cm (2 in.) up from the bottom and fit the tap. Put the wire mesh behind the back of the tap to prevent it getting clogged and drill a few small holes in the bin lid so that the worms can get some air. Put around 10 cm (4 in.) sand or gravel in the bottom of the bin and lay the pieces of wood on top, then dampen the shredded newspaper or straw and put a 10 cm (4 in.) layer of that on top of the wood. Make a hole in the centre of the layer of newspaper and gently add the composting worms.

WHAT DO THE WORMS EAT?

Basically the worms love certain types of food waste. As long as it's finely chopped they'll eat fruit, vegetable peelings, bread, cereal, coffee grounds as well as green leaves. They don't like meat and fish or cheese, rice or pasta or huge piles of grass cuttings. Bury the scraps in the layer of newspaper or straw.

Beware of overfeeding the worms: only replenish food supplies in small batches when you can see that they have finished the last meal you gave them, otherwise the wormery will rot and smell.

WHAT DO I GET IN RETURN?

After a few weeks, turn on the tap and out will pour very concentrated fertilizer, which you must dilute with 10 parts water before feeding your plants. After a few months, remove the worms and use the contents of the wormery as compost on your plants, then refill the wormery as above and put the worms back in.

TROUBLESHOOTING

- If the worms collect on the bottom of the wormery lid it usually means your worms are hungry or unhappy for some reason (too much food, too wet, too dry, too much fresh green matter – such as grass cuttings – that heats up as it decomposes). Make sure you fix the problem and they will settle down again.

- Flies in the wormery won't hurt it, but to keep them at bay keep a lid on the wormery and make sure that your food waste is covered by the wet shredded newspaper.

- If lots of tiny white worms appear, don't worry. These do a similar job to the composting worms but generally appear when the wormery is becoming waterlogged. Check your drainage and add more shredded newspaper as necessary.

Try growing some mushrooms

Very easy to grow indoors or out, kids find growing mushrooms fascinating, and if you're lucky they'll like the taste of them too. The easiest thing to do is to buy a mushroom growing kit that consists of mushroom spawn and the right mix of compost in a tub.

However, mushroom spawn is available separately, and it's easy to grow mushrooms on your lawn especially if you have a wilder area in the garden. Pick a warm damp day between late spring and early autumn and, using a trowel, lift small squares of turf about 5 cm (2 in.) thick and 30 cm (12 in.) apart. Place a walnut-size piece of spawn into each hole and replace the turf. You should see mushrooms growing through in about 10–12 weeks.

Some old gardening tips

Growing tomatoes

Wet some compost and compress it into 5 cm (2 in.) cubes. Make a dimple in the top of the cube and put one tomato seed in the dimple. When it germinates, let it grow until its roots show at the side of the block. Transfer into 10 cm (4 in.) pots and grow on until ready for planting out.

When the plants are growing, every time you pass them give them a little stroke. This will condition them into thinking it is windy and consequently the plant will develop short, strong stems, which will make them better able to cope with the bumper crop you hope for!

Feeding Tomato Plants

Fill a water butt or dustbin with water and add as many nettles as will go in it. Leave it to soak for 3 to 4 weeks until it smells like strong manure, then – wearing gloves – take out the nettles, leaving the smelly liquid in the bin. When the first tomatoes have set, water weekly with this liquid which is rich in potassium and produces healthy organic fruit. Peppers can be grown and treated in the same way.

Chitting your spuds

Set your seed potatoes to chit in old egg boxes and place them in a warm spot. Egg boxes seem made for this job and will support the potato as the shoots grow.

New potatoes

For extra-early potatoes, add grass from your first lawn cutting of the year to your potato trench. Once you have dug your trench, place the seed potato in the trench, add a little farmyard manure or compost and cover with a little soil. Then fill the trench with grass cuttings, tread down well and cover with the rest of the soil from the trench. The grass will start to decompose, emitting heat, and warming the soil in the trench, giving the potatoes a good start.

Fruit trees

Keep the area around the trunk of the tree well dug over, especially in the spring. This lets the birds get at the bugs that over-winter in the ground and want to climb up the tree in spring to lay their eggs in the newly formed fruit.

Apple picking

To tell if an apple is ready for picking, cup it in your hand and gently twist the stem. If it comes away from the branch easily, it's ripe.

Guttered!

When you are planting seeds for a row of salad or peas for example, use a length of guttering about 60 cm (2 ft) long to plant the seeds in. Fill your guttering with peat-free compost and press it down firmly. Sow the seeds evenly along the length. When they are ready to plant out, dig a shallow trench the same length as the guttering and simply slide the row of seedlings into the trench.

The humble bumble

You can do something about the declining bee population we hear about in the media: buy a bee box for your garden. These smallish boxes contain two compartments, one for the queen bee and the other for her workers. If you put the box in a warm, sheltered spot (not in direct sunlight), preferably near a flower bed or hedge so they have a good source of food nearby, you'll be doing the bee population *and* your garden a big favour.

It stings!

If you are stung by a bee, apply a paste of bicarbonate of soda and water. Bee stings are acid, and the paste should help soothe the sting. On the other hand, wasp or hornet stings are alkaline, so the acid of lemon juice or vinegar will help.

An effective soother for insect bites is to squeeze a marigold leaf and rub it on the spot. It's well worth growing a few marigolds in any garden, both for their soothing properties and their cheery colour.

The herb garden

Herbs are a valuable addition to any garden. They provide flavouring, aroma and decoration; they can be used for remedies, infusions and beauty treatments; and they attract butterflies and bees.

The wide range of herbs – from trees and shrubs to smaller plants – means that they can be grown in different parts of the garden, between paving stones, for example, on lawns or in containers. However, if you have space it is worth creating a separate herb garden with easy access to the kitchen. The choice of herbs is a matter of personal taste, but my selection would include sage, chives, mint (which is best grown in pots buried in the soil to prevent the roots spreading), basil, thyme, parsley, rosemary, fennel (very tall and probably better at the back of a herbaceous border), lemon balm and oregano. Most herbs are fragrant with attractive flowers and foliage and when grouped together make a heady impact on the senses.

I've grown my herbs, now what?

Apart from having a fragrant pot of herbs growing and thriving, you can use your herbs for lots of things. See pages 46–9 for some culinary uses for many of our favourite herbs. The first thing, though, is to harvest and store them properly.

Harvesting, drying, freezing and storing your herbs

You have laboured long and hard over your herb pots or kitchen garden, so don't let your work go to waste. Make sure you harvest your herbs at their best and you can store or freeze them for enjoying later in the year.

Harvesting

Pick your herbs for everyday use whenever you need them, but for storing herbs the main harvest should take place in the late summer and autumn (according to whether leaves or seeds are wanted). The first harvesting should be just before the herbs come into flower. Cut herbs back to about one-third of their growth at each cutting and then allow them to recover before the next cutting. Leaves should be cut on stems.

Try to harvest herbs when the sun has dried off the dew or rain, but before the full heat of the sun starts to extract too much herbal fragrance.

- ✖ Tarragon should be cut when young, at about 30 cm (1 ft) tall, otherwise the leaves may be bitter.

- ✖ Sage can be cut from early spring to late autumn.

- ✖ Rosemary is best cut in late summer.

- ✖ Bay can be cut all year round but mature leaves dry best.

- ✖ Borage, camomile flowers and marigold petals are dried.

- ✖ Dill, anise, caraway and coriander should be left until seed heads ripen, although the leaves can be used for flavouring throughout the summer.

- ✖ Garlic bulbs should be lifted when the leaves are dead.

Drying

LEAVES

All leaves should be dried on their stems. Pick stems of herbs, tie them in small bunches and hang the bunches in a warm, dark, dry, well-ventilated place. The only exception to this is bay leaves, which should be taken off their stems and laid out for drying. Make sure you label each bunch of herbs so that you know what you have when they are dry. When dried, rub the leaves away from their stems and store them in small dark glass jars in a cool dry place. Label the jars and date them – dried herbs should be used within a year as their flavour does deteriorate gradually. Parsley doesn't dry well in my experience, so it's best to freeze that.

FLOWERS AND PETALS

Pick them dry and fully open but not wilted or discoloured. Handle the flowers gently and spread them out on muslin-covered racks to dry, so that air can circulate freely around them. Rose petals and stems of lavender can also be dried in this way for use in pot pourri or lavender bags.

SEEDS

Caraway, coriander, dill, anise and fennel seeds are ready to harvest when the seed capsules turn brown. Cut off the whole seed head about halfway down the stem and tie the stems together in bunches. Put a paper bag over the bunch of seed heads and hang them in a cool dry place until the seeds have fallen into the paper bag. Spread the seeds on trays, cover them with a piece of paper and leave to dry for about two weeks before putting them into airtight jars. To test whether they are completely dry, try to break one with your fingernail, they should be hard.

Freezing

Tender-leaved herbs like mint, parsley and basil are much better frozen than dried, and by far the best method is to chop your herbs finely and pack them into ice-cube trays, adding a little water to cover. Freeze the whole tray, then tap the cubes out of the tray and pack them into polythene bags for freezer storage. Then, when you need that herb for a soup or stew, the whole cube can be added to your dish.

The kiss of the sun for pardon,
The song of the birds for mirth,
You are nearer God's heart in a garden
Than anywhere else on earth.

From 'God's Garden' by Dorothy Gurney (1858–1932)

This little poem, often found on plaques in gardens, sums up the serenity one feels in the peace and quiet of a garden.

The weather and weather forecasting

As anyone who works the land knows, success is largely dependent on the weather. These days there are short-range forecasts, long-range forecasts, all sorts of predictions, all done by scientists working with sophisticated knowledge and equipment.

There are also amateur forecasters who use knowledge that has passed down to them, who have reasonable success in predicting short- and long-term forecasts. These are often based on observations of the countryside around them – the hedgerows, the sky, the movements of birds and animals and the like.

At one time most homes would have a barometer hanging on the wall, which would be tapped every day to see if the arrow went up, indicating high pressure and fine weather, or down, indicating low pressure and cloud or rain. These seem to have fallen out of fashion now, but they are reliable indicators of changes in the weather.

Red sky at night

Here are some weather-based sayings that were passed down the generations to me. Whether they're accurate or not, they are certainly fun to say:

> Red sky at night, shepherd's delight,
> Red sky in the morning, shepherd's warning.
>
> Mackerel sky, mackerel sky,
> Not long wet and not long dry.

Rain before seven,
Dry after eleven.

One swallow does not make a summer.

If March comes in like a lion
It will go out like a lamb.
If it comes in like a lamb,
It will go out like a lion

Haloes round the sun or moon,
Rain or snow soon

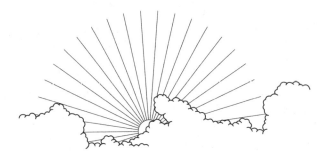

Weather and wildlife

Some animals and plants are sensitive to environmental conditions and react accordingly:

❄ Some flowers, such as tulips, daisies and dandelions, close their petals before a storm to protect the pollen in the flower.

- Pine cones close up before a storm to protect the seeds (and I have seen pine cones strung together and made into little figures for use as weather indicators).

- Bees stay close to the hive when it's going to rain because nectar gathering is more difficult for them in the rain.

- A fisherman friend always says, 'Fish bite the least when the wind's in the east', and apparently there is some truth in that. In a dry east wind the insects that fish eat fly too far above the surface for fish to catch them.

- When hawthorn blossoms are plentiful a severe winter will follow.

- A profusion of blackberries in the hedgerows heralds a harsh winter.

- Swallows flying low may indicate air pressure is dropping.

- A piece of seaweed hung outside will feel damp in humid weather because its coating of sea salt absorbs moisture.

- Frogs call before the rain
  But in the sun are quiet again.

Building a log store

Having an open fireplace or a wood-burning stove requires having a handy supply of seasoned logs. A wood store at its simplest is just a pile of wood covered by a tarpaulin but, for practical purposes, it is better to have an organized, purpose-built store that is well located for stocking up the log basket. A purpose-built log store can look attractive in a garden. Seeing it in the autumn, with enough logs to last the winter, neatly stacked, row upon row, gives you a warm feeling of satisfaction. It must be the 'hunter-gatherer' instinct in me!

Like sheds, log stores are available in kit form ready for erection or they can be made from recycled wood. I made mine from five wooden pallets, which facilitate the circulation of air. The structure has two pallets laid flat with three uprights, one at each end and one in the middle, giving two adjacent stores. These are nailed together, along with strengthening planks across the back. Three wooden planks are nailed across the top, again one at each end and one down the middle. The roof needs a slope of at least 15 degrees and is better if it overhangs the lower end to avoid rain dripping on the logs. After putting on a wooden roof, finish with shed felt to keep the logs dry. My store is close to a wall that shelters it from the prevailing wind and rain.

Enjoying the garden

Entertaining

Eating out in the garden is one of summer's great pleasures whether it be breakfast, lunch, afternoon tea or an evening meal. The sights and scents of the garden combined with the freshness of seasonal foods and herbs (perhaps the produce of your own garden) can create an enduring experience. In the evening, as the long shadows fall with the setting sun, the candlelight that illuminates the patio and surrounding trees and shrubs creates a magical atmosphere to be enjoyed by family and friends.

Burnt offerings

Praise be to the barbecue, whose wonderful tempting aromas waft across the evening breeze from your neighbours' gardens. Barbecue season is when the male of the species comes into his own, all kitted out in his chef's hat and apron, serving up succulent charcoal-grilled steaks, sizzling sausages (not burnt) and tasty pieces of chicken breast on skewers, previously marinated in something deliciously spicy.

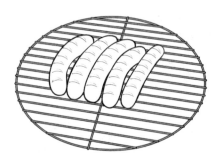

However, I'm sorry to say that this Grandfather has little wisdom to offer on the subject of barbecuing. My carbon-flavoured, burnt offerings find little favour with the recipients. Still, as children say when being questioned on their school reports, 'You can't be good at everything!' In my mind, the wise grandad is the one who sits back with a glass of something refreshing and lets the others get on with it!

The easier option

It really is much easier to cook indoors, but eat 'al fresco', particularly if you abandon the chef's hat! The fare cooked inside – tasty quiches, honey-glazed baked ham, studded with cloves, salmon poached in white wine and herbs, garnished with lemon and parsley, and served with avocado and crème fraiche sauce – provides a welcome change from barbecue food for your guests. This can be accompanied by lovely fresh salads from the garden and baby new potatoes cooked with mint, the aroma of which has wafted through the kitchen window, been caught by the breeze and carried into your neighbour's garden ... 'Bon Appetit!'

Relaxing in the garden

Rudyard Kipling wrote in his poem 'The Glory of the Garden', 'Gardens are not made ... by sitting in the shade.' It is sometimes easier said than done to find time to relax in the garden. No sooner have you settled down than you notice something that needs your attention. If you think hard enough, though, you can find an adequate excuse to justify a lazy afternoon. As the humorist James Dent wrote, 'A perfect summer day is when the sun is shining, the breeze is blowing, the birds are singing … and the lawnmower is broken.'

Summertime and the pleasure of enjoying the sunshine is an opportunity that should not be missed. With our climate, summer could be here today and gone tomorrow. So, seize the day and say, as I do, 'A garden is more fun … when relaxing in the sun.' (After Kipling)

Let Play Commence!

Here is a selection of the activities we have enjoyed on days out with the grandchildren. Whether you go to the seaside or on a trip to the park, a bit of a run around can make everyone feel so much better. Taking deep breaths of oxygen at the seaside, like breathing in mountain and countryside air, in itself gives a sense of well-being.

At the beach or in the park

- Beach cricket – It is amazing how soon this activity attracts 'joiners-in' and new friends are made. Play with a tennis ball and one or two batsmen according to numbers. If you hit it in the sea you are out.

✖ Football cricket – Use a large inflated plastic ball or beach ball. Bowl from ten paces at the wicket. A run is scored by running to a mark ten paces away from the side of the wicket, after the ball has been kicked or headed. Players are out if they handle the ball, are caught, or bowled.

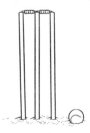

✖ Hand tennis – Mark out a court in the sand with a stick (size will depend on number of players, but no more than four a side). Draw a line across the court to divide into two equal parts. Use a football-sized plastic ball and serve from behind the baseline with the hand. The ball must only bounce once on either side and must be hit over the central line and stay in the court. Score as in tennis.

✖ Tag – Mark out a restricted area as above. A player touched by Grandpa is 'on' and must chase to touch another player who then becomes the chaser. All players must stay in the restricted area.

✖ Dodge ball – If there are enough players, divide them into two teams. One team forms a circle and the other team run around within the circle, dodging the plastic ball thrown by the people forming the circle. If you are hit below the knee then you join the circle. The last one left in the centre is the winner.

- Sand golf – Use sandcastle buckets or empty ice cream tubs sunk in the sand and build a few obstacles. For a club use the handle end of a spade or a piece of driftwood or, if nothing else is available, use a clenched fist.

- Quoits – Try to throw the rope or rubber ring over a pin poking out of the ground a set distance away.

- Rounders – Mark out the pitch using anything you have to hand for posts – towels or buckets will do. Use a bat or racquet and a tennis ball.

- Six passes – Divide players into two teams. Six consecutive passes by a team scores one goal. The opposing team try to intercept and gain control of the ball. If the ball touches the ground start the counting again.

- Tip and Run – Cricket but with only one batsman, who must run every time the ball is struck. The bowler can bowl as soon as the ball is received from the fielders but it must be bowled from behind the bowling mark. Use a tennis ball.

- French cricket – The batsman must defend the legs below the knee and must not move his or her feet. The ball is bowled and if hit, bowled from where the ball is fielded. The ball can be passed but only to a player behind the batsman. The batsman can be caught out or bowled out by being hit below the knee.

✂ Ducks and drakes – also known as stone skimming or stone skipping. I was surprised to learn that the world record, set by Kurt Steiner in Pennsylvania in 2002, was forty skims – that's an incredible forty times the flat stone skims over the water and hops up into the air again! There is a technique to doing it well, but children the world over love having a go at this game.

✂ Boules, bocce, petanque – Call it what you will, but the good old-fashioned bowling of a bigger ball at a smaller 'jack' is a very easy game to set up. The object is to land your ball closer to the jack or strike the jack and move it towards your other balls (or at least away from your opponents').

These games can be as easy or as strenuous as you choose, and offer opportunities for stretching and strengthening for everyone. They can be enjoyed by young and old alike, whether taking part or organizing the action. Simply make sure that you work within your own ability and stamina and don't overdo it.

Garden games

It is always wise to have a few games up your sleeve (or prepared earlier) when there are children to be entertained. Here are a few well-tried competitions, ideally with small prizes for everyone.

✖ Treasure hunt is a simple game with small prizes hidden away for the seekers to find. To make it more difficult set a trail of clues (some help can be given to the younger ones).

✖ Set up a series of games rather like a garden fete. Skittles using empty bean cans and tennis balls; 'throw a ball into a bucket', using a tilted bucket propped up against a block of wood (vary the distance the ball has to be thrown); knocking tin cans off an easily constructed shelf etc.

✖ Play bowls by taking it in turns to roll a ball close to the target placed a distance away.

✖ Catching game – if you drop a catch, you go down on one knee, drop another, two knees, drop three catches, you lose a hand, etc. A successful catch reverses the process. But remember: the smaller the children the larger the ball.

✖ Children stand in a circle round an adult. The adult throws a large ball to a child, taking each child in turn. If it is dropped a penalty is paid. In the next round the hands must be clapped before catching or a penalty is paid. If the hands are clapped when the ball is not passed (Grandpa's dummy pass) again a penalty is paid.

- Follow the leader and do what the leader does (giant strides, small steps, funny walks) and follow wherever the leader goes.

Grandfathers who are able to exercise with their grandchildren are creating a tradition of activity, and children who have been active while young are more likely to continue being active in later life.

Card games

Fantastic for whiling away a winter's night or getting the kids away from the TV or games console for a while, having a few card games up your sleeve is a great way for the family to have fun together.

Go Fish

This is an exciting game of chance and skill for two or more players – and it's fun to see older children developing the memory skill as they enjoy playing it.

If two or three people are playing, the dealer deals seven cards each; if more, only five cards each, with the rest of the cards being placed face down in the middle of the table to form the 'fish' pile.

Players sort their cards into groups of the same number or the same picture, making sure no other players see their hand. To start, the player to the left of the dealer picks any other player and asks for cards of any one of the groups in his own hand – for example, if he holds two aces, he might ask the other player for aces. If the other player has a card that's been requested, he has to hand it over. If the player does not have the cards he's been asked for, he tells the requester to 'go fish'. The requester then has to take a card from the top of the fish pile, and the person who told him to 'go fish' becomes the requester. Any player who collects all four cards in a group – all four twos, all four knaves, etc – puts them face down in front of him.

The winner is the first player to have nothing but a collection of complete sets in front of him. If two players run out of cards together, the winner is the one with the most complete sets.

Old Maid

This is a good game for younger children and is for three or more people. Take a deck of cards and remove one of the queens, leaving a pair of queens in one colour and a single queen – the Old Maid herself.

All cards are dealt, face down, and then, keeping their cards hidden from other players, the players sort their cards into matching pairs of the same number or picture, putting down their matches face up in front of them. If any player has three matching cards, two should be put down, while the third card stays in his hand; if anyone has four matching cards, two pairs are laid down.

The player to the left of the dealer fans his cards out so that he can see them but no one else can, and offers them to the player on his left, who takes out a random card from the fan. If the picked card matches any cards he already has, he puts down the pair. If not, he keeps it in his hand. Then he offers his fanned cards to the next player. This goes on until all the cards have been put down in pairs – except for the Old Maid, the only card that cannot be paired. The player left holding this card loses the game.

Snap

The classic card game for children everywhere, you can play this with special 'snap' cards or with an ordinary deck of cards (although two decks are better if you are playing with more than three players).

Shuffle the cards well and deal them all out. Players do not look at their cards, but hold them in a stack, face down. The player on the left of the dealer turns over his top card and places it next to his own pile. The next player does the same, starting a new pile of his own. This goes on until a player sees that two cards on top of any of the face-up piles are the same, and shouts 'snap!' The first player to do so takes all the cards in the matching face-up piles and adds them to the bottom of his face-down pile. The game continues with the player to the left of the winner.

If a player calls 'snap!' incorrectly, he pays every player one card from his face-down pile. The winner is the player who ends up with all the cards.

An easier variation for younger children is to play the game with one central pool of cards rather than individual piles. Players add one card to the central pool until the top card matches the one beneath it. The first person to shout 'snap!' takes the whole pile of cards and adds them to the bottom of his stack.

Beggar My Neighbour

This game is for two or three players and is best played fast! Deal out all 52 cards in the deck, face down, no peeking. The person to the left of the dealer starts by placing his top card face up in the centre of the table and the game then moves round clockwise, each player adding one card face up to the pile until someone turns up a picture card (an ace, king, queen or knave). The player who turned up the picture card then demands payment from his neighbour, the next player:

> Four cards for an ace
> Three cards for a king
> Two cards for a queen
> One card for a knave

These cards are placed on the central pile. If, however, a picture card is turned up as one of the payment cards, the turn goes on to the next player to the left, who then has to pay the required number of cards, and so on. This goes on until the payment is complete, without a picture card being turned up. The last player who turned up a picture card takes the whole pile and puts it at the bottom of his cards and play begins again.

The winner is the player who uses up all his cards.

A Grandfather's Job

When I started writing this book I asked my grandchildren for their help in various ways. One thing I asked them to do was to note down the things they enjoyed doing with me when they were younger, and their answers were quite revealing. I realized that the moments that were important to them, I hadn't even remembered; and occasions I thought they would have remembered, for various reasons, hardly got a mention. One of the most important memories that constantly came up in the answers was how special they were made to feel – 'showing me how precious and clever I am'.

We live in a materialistic world and grandparents can easily fall into the trap of indulging their grandchildren with expensive gifts and treats. However, the most valuable thing you can give them is your time. Having eleven grandchildren, it's not easy to share my time equally, but the important thing is to make sure that the time that each child spends with you is quality time, and that each grandchild feels special. You will find that as your grandchildren grow, your relationship with them changes and develops too.

Grandfather and his many hats

Throughout his grandchildren's lives Grandfather can help to enhance their development – physical, mental, emotional and social – assuming different roles at different stages and yet again more roles for the different areas of responsibility he accepts. He has many hats to wear.

Grandad the carer

- Somehow Grandad's frame lends itself to giving cuddles – the most natural reaction for a tiny baby when put into Grandad's arms is to fall asleep, and the most natural reaction for Grandad when cuddling a grandchild is to fall asleep with it (luckily Mum is close by). Of course, when it's nappy-changing time baby is handed back, Grandad never did get the hang of that!

- Taking the baby for a walk in the pram or buggy and giving Mum a break is always appreciated.

- Caring for a toddler is quite a test on Grandad's resourcefulness. It is here that he dons his entertainer's hat (see page 145).

- When the grandchildren start primary school, since many mothers work these days, the caring role can change to after-school care, but you just have to remember to watch the clock and be ready to do the taxi run. School-holiday care is also helpful to working mums but is best if used in conjunction with a holiday club. Grandfathers do have a life!

- As the children move through secondary school they think they are too grown up for Grandad's care but, when on their own at home, a discreet phone call to them can set the mind at rest. Of course if they are ill it's a different matter and TLC is very welcome.

Grandfather the entertainer

This is one of Grandad's most important and enjoyable roles. He is expected to have something up his sleeve for every occasion and to meet every crisis. His 'bag of tricks' contains amusing diversions for babies through to teenagers. Here are some games that follow the progression through the various stages of development.

EARLY DAYS

- Peep Bo – A traditional game for babies that never ceases to arouse chuckles.

- Round and Round the Garden like a Teddy Bear – with laughter evoked by a tickle under the arm at the end.

- Humpty Dumpty from the old nursery rhyme. When 'Humpty Dumpty has a great fall', both baby and Grandad are amused. The older the baby the more excited Grandad is allowed to get and the further baby drops between his knees.

- Babies become more interesting to grandpas as they develop and begin to react to stimuli such as the many different noises around them, and especially those made by Grandpa, such as animal noises, vehicle noises, clocks, singing etc. As they begin to sit up and crawl, desirable objects can be placed for them to reach, and they can be encouraged to identify sounds and recognize everyday things from cards or picture books.

TODDLERHOOD

- At the toddler stage, children begin to become curious and get into everything, opening cupboard doors, delving into boxes and tasting everything that comes their way. A wooden spoon and a biscuit tin provide a lot of entertainment for the child, somewhat less for Grandad.

- Playing with the wrapping paper and boxes that presents come in, rather than the present itself, is the norm for young children. Grandad really comes into his own now – fun time! Grandad is expected to endlessly pull or push the present box around the floor with the child in it – sometimes it's a car, sometimes a train, sometimes an aeroplane and everyone has fun with the appropriate sounds. Why bother with the expense of the present?

- Bumpity-bump – shows how to come downstairs safely, sitting, not standing as adults do. Sitting on Grandad's knee to begin with and then sitting side by side as we bump down each step at a time, chanting bumpity-bump, bumpity-bump.

- Throwing and catching balls of screwed-up paper or soft toys. Larger balls are easier to catch and the game helps to develop hand-eye coordination.

- Guess which hand? – moving things from hand to hand (small ball of screwed-up paper or similar) and guessing which hand it is in. There are many tricks to use to deceive the eye.

- Writing down a number and asking the child to make a picture out of it (for example a 2 is easily changed into a duck or swan, and a 4 makes a lovely sailing boat). This is a tried and tested diversionary tactic when waiting for a meal to arrive in a restaurant. The child is well occupied and the napkins become more interesting at the same time.

- Jumping – children love to see how high they can jump. As they get older they love jokes. A favourite is, 'I can jump higher than a house' and on being challenged to do so, Grandad gives a little jump. 'That's not higher than a house,' they say. 'It is,' says Grandad, 'Houses can't jump! Ha, ha!'

SCHOOLDAYS

- It is at school age when the demands of grandchildren are at their most exhausting, particularly if you are entertaining more than one at the same time. It is also the period when their memories are the most vivid. It is lovely re-living all the exciting times with them through their recollections and wondering where I got all my energy from! Making dens both inside and out is one such activity using anything that is handy, ranging from cushions from the sofa and chairs, clothes horse and old sheets, to a tarpaulin slung over a plank between two trees to make a tent, along with all the necessary equipment for living. A campfire at the end of the day with jacket potatoes, toasted marshmallows and campfire songs finishes the day off nicely. No wonder I was tired!

- Sometimes grandchildren are quite happy to let Grandad sit back and they will entertain him and Grandma. They love putting on a concert. After much planning, whispering, arguing and practising, the dressing-up box is ransacked, a programme is produced and we are in our seats. We are treated to a medley of dancing, singing, playing of instruments, comedy turns, poems, charades and I don't know what else because it is always bedtime before it has finished.

Grandfather the storyteller and poet

When Grandad has come back from the bookshop or the library with his books, a pile quickly appears by his side ready to read, and an attentive audience is there ready to listen. As with other roles this develops as each grandchild gets older.

A GOOD READ

- Young children love looking at picture books, talking about what is happening, and making up their own stories. For my grandchildren, best of all at bedtime are Grandpa's own 'White Duck' stories about his own real white duck that lives on his pond. White Duck has many adventures and gets into lots of scrapes but in the end he always saves the day (as a good hero should).

- These days it is possible to buy personalized books, in which the child and their siblings and friends feature. However, it's much more appealing to them to make their own book. It is easy to turn a drawing book into a house shape, decorating the front to look like their home. Every alternate page inside has a window cut into it that will open and close. Behind each window a photograph of each member of the family including pets and favourite toys can be stuck (or the child can do a drawing if they are able). Under the photo or drawing write the name in large clear print. Here you have a first reading book, the child soon memorizing each single word, however long, by its distinctive shape. It will become a firm favourite.

✹ A walk in a wood can become more interesting if it is a walk to Pooh Bear's 'Hundred Acre Wood'. Even better if you have a Pooh Bear or a Piglet to take with you (toy or imaginary) to hide in a tree. The grand-children can relive the story on their walk through the woods, soaking up the atmosphere and looking for the characters and their homes. Remember to take the camera with you, as photographs of these jaunts will provide endless enjoyment for years to come.

✹ Grandpa's Midnight Feasts often occur around seven in the evening at our house – curtains closed, candles lit, time for stories. Everyone in a circle on the floor, the atmosphere building up, hearts a-flutter, someone starts the story and then on to the next one to continue, no one knowing what is going to happen or how it will end. Then it's finished, everyone scared out of their wits, and time for the feast. The menu contains only things that children like to eat and drink. The only adult in on the secret is Grandpa! The best time to organize a GMF is when grandchildren are staying over and Grandma is out for the evening.

POEMS TO REMEMBER

Children enjoy poetry and songs almost from birth. Poetry appreciation changes as the child develops:

✹ As babies they respond to lullabies, falling asleep to the strains of 'Rock-a-Bye-Baby' or 'Hush Little Baby Don't Say a Word'.

- Action Rhymes follow with children doing the actions, for example:

  Incy, Wincy Spider climbed up the waterspout,
  (use fingers to climb up slowly)
  Down came the rain and washed poor spider out,
  (fingers run down quickly)
  Out came the sunshine and dried up all the rain,
  (arms make sun, then fingers wriggle up)
  Then Incy, Wincy Spider climbed up the spout again.
  (fingers climb up slowly)

- There are also Nursery Rhymes, which allow children to do the actions and join in with the chorus and rhyming words, for example:

  Five little ducks swam out one day,
  (*hold five fingers up*)
  Over the pond and far away,
  (fingers make a swimming movement)
  Mother Duck called 'Quack, quack, quack'
  But only four little ducks came swimming back.
  (*put one finger down and 'swim' the others*)

  The rhyme goes on in the same way until there is only one finger left up, (It's best to leave Mother Duck with one duckling rather than none – it saves the tears!)

- Children also enjoy personalized poems, either composed for them or written jointly with Grandpa. It is easy to pick out a simple metre. Writing together can encourage children to write their own poems as they get older, often with surprising results.

Grandfather the first-aider

With all the adventures, trying new skills, and the rough and tumble of play and discovery, it is inevitable that there are bumps, cuts, bruises and sprains or breaks. Reassurance and assessment are the first steps to take before applying first aid and deciding if more advanced treatment is necessary.

From my experience, a handy first-aid box should contain these essential items:

✖ Grandad's magic cream (antiseptic) and spray

✖ Strips of plasters – to cut to required size; box of plasters

✖ Low adherent dressing pads –absorbent and sterile

✖ A pair of scissors

✖ Antiseptic wipes

✖ Bandages

✖ A sling

✖ Safety pins

✖ Micropore tape

✖ Cotton wool

✖ Plastic gloves to prevent transfer of germs

Grandfather the mentor

Life is one long learning experience. Children think that learning is something that happens at school but we as grandparents know that it is a continuous process. Grandad, therefore, needs to take advantage of opportunities that arise to pass on his wisdom to his grandchildren. Without their realizing it he can put on his 'mentor hat' while they are out walking, in the car, working in the garden, having a discussion at family meals and on countless other occasions. Grandad's teaching opportunities change as the child grows up.

OUT AND ABOUT

When out walking with babies or toddlers in prams or buggies the walk is much more interesting for the child when he or she has an awareness of its surroundings. This can be stimulated by:

- ✄ Talking about animals in the fields, the sounds they make, what the baby animals are called.

- ✄ Watching out for traffic, its sound, colour, large or small, fast or slow, how many wheels.

- ✄ Observing the weather – hot, cold, rainy, sunny etc. Puddles, snowmen shadows etc. Weather rhymes.

- ✄ Who is missing – talking about family members and where they are – at home, at school, at work etc.

IN THE CAR

Long boring car journeys lend themselves to a bit of surreptitious educating along with passing the time and keeping the peace. Gear the game to the age group in the car. These activities can include:

- The old favourite 'I Spy', saying whether it is inside or outside the car.

- Rhyming Riddles where someone (usually an adult) makes up a rhyming riddle omitting the last word, which the children have to guess. For example, 'I know a word that rhymes with dish, It lives in the sea and it's a ****,' or 'I know a flower that rhymes with lazy, it has white petals and it's a *****.'

- Last Letter. A topic is chosen – it can be girls' or boys' names, towns, flowers – anything. The youngest in the car chooses a topic for example, boys' names, and says the first name, for example, Martin then, going clockwise round the car, the next one has to say a boy's name beginning with the last letter of the previous one, for example Neil, the next one might say Len. When the game is stuck, change to another topic. The rules are very flexible!

- Animals – collective nouns (a 'herd' of cattle, a 'pod' of whales), the names of the male, female and baby of the species.

- Geography Quiz – countries, capital cities, rivers etc.

- An old favourite with me is People's Initials. This works well if you have a large extended family and you can include cousins, aunts and uncles, etc. Someone starts with the initials of a member of the family (first name and surname) and when someone guesses it, it is their turn.

NEVER TOO OLD FOR HOMEWORK

Children can research just about anything they want to these days on the Internet, but there is nothing quite like tapping Grandad's knowledge when it comes to history (not always first-hand knowledge, of course) So when the phone rings in the late afternoon, I know I am in for some 'telephone homework'.

I am quite pleased I'm not called upon to help with maths homework. There are, however, times when I am presented with maths challenges brought home from school. I usually get out of that tricky situation by saying, 'I think Grandma would be interested in that.'

TEENS AND BEYOND

As grandchildren move higher up in their secondary school and then on to further education or into the workplace, the role of mentor adapts to a very flexible, elusive kind of supporting role that can be called upon as and when it is required.

This indefinable role includes:

- Being a good listener.
- Being able to judge whether advice is being sought or not.
- Knowing if you are equipped to give advice.
- If not, knowing where to direct the grandchild for advice.
- Being able to discuss issues in an unbiased manner and appreciate their point of view.
- Helping them to realize the importance of questioning opinions rather than just accepting them and being brainwashed.

AND SUDDENLY THEY'RE ADULTS

As grandchildren move out into the wider world they become more independent, living their lives away from the family, and understandably Grandad sees less of them. His experience and wisdom can still be of use to the young person starting out in life. He is always willing to:

- Discuss courses they are doing.
- Listen to their hopes and ambitions for the future.
- Offer to help with job applications.

✖ Give advice on job interviews – how to prepare, and the correct dress code.

✖ Talk about work issues.

✖ Show by example the wisdom of living within one's means As Mr Micawber advised in Dickens's, *David Copperfield*:

> Annual income twenty pounds/
>
> Annual expenditure nineteen pounds, nineteen and six – result happiness.
>
> Annual income twenty pounds
>
> Annual expenditure twenty pounds and sixpence – result misery.

Grandfather the confidant

There are times when grandchildren like someone to talk to other than their parents, and if a relationship of trust has been built up by sharing little secrets, the grandchildren are happy to treat Grandad as a confidant. In being taken into confidence most secrets are kept as secrets unless Grandfather exercises his judgement differently, that is, if he thinks the issue warrants it.

Small children are not discerning in any way and tell their grandad (and their teacher) all sorts of tales about friends and family, (things that might well embarrass their parents if they knew). It is best to let such confidences go in one ear and straight out the other.

Other confidences often require much more attention such as:

❋ Bullying – This is one issue that needs to be dealt with promptly because of the devastating effect it can have on the victim. If you feel that a grandchild has been the subject of bullying, mention your concern to the parents, who should arrange a meeting with the head-teacher or a teacher responsible for pastoral care. All schools have an anti-bullying policy, which will give steps to take to resolve the problem. The important thing is that the child is able to talk to someone who will take the problem seriously. The outcome always needs to be followed up.

❋ Friendships – Some children have a best friend, others prefer to be part of a group and others are always on the edge of a group, but, whichever is the case, friendships are vitally important to children's well-being. Things can go wrong in friendships and when this happens it can seem like the end of the world to the child. Grandad can usually detect when things are not running smoothly and needs to tap on his wisdom and experience to help. The most important thing he can do is to listen, which can help the child, as he or she talks, to put things into perspective. Hopefully the child can see that things are not as bad as he or she thought and can move on with confidence.

- Marriage break-ups – With such a high proportion of marriages breaking up these days, Grandfather can be a lifeline to grandchildren whose lives have been turned upside down. Children are often unwittingly drawn into the parental turmoil and Grandad can be a stabilizing influence in their lives – someone to turn to for unstinting support.

- Growing up – It is the opinion these days, that on reaching their teens children can become monsters. Despite there being a double generation gap, relationships between grandfather and grandchild can flourish during these often problematic years. If Grandad comes over as someone who's not easily shocked, as someone they can share a joke with (even if it is slightly risqué), or as someone who isn't always harping back to 'my day' and tries, above all to remember what it was like to be young, then the teenage grandchild might still confide in him and even come to him for advice.

- Despite today's enlightened approach, children who are growing up still have questions that need a frank answer. Answers and advice need to be honest with explanations truthful and to the point. It is always flattering when Grandad is approached with these problems and is a reflection on the trust built up over the years.

Being a grandfather is a very privileged position, one to be taken seriously, cherished and enjoyed. The joys and responsibilities of being a grandfather go hand in hand: one complements the other. How much responsibility a grandfather is able to take on depends on many factors, but the joy one gains from one's grandchildren is directly related to the relationships built up over the years, through the responsibilities one is able and willing to accept.